The —
LITTLE BOOK OF
ANTHROPOLOGY

Rasha Barrage

Contents

Introduction

"Where are you from?" On face value, this seems like quite a straightforward question. But the query itself suggests a recognition of *difference*, and the answer could range from the street where you live to your place of birth, or it could go way back to the origin of your ancestors. Until the twentieth century, this question was reserved for the wealthiest and most powerful in the world: those who had the resources and privilege to travel and meet people far from where they considered "home." In the twenty-first century, this question is asked so regularly that we can easily overlook its significance and the breadth of its possible meanings —unless you think like an anthropologist. Curiosity, comparison and connection are what inspire anthropology, and its endless quest to understand our origin and what it means to be human—across countries, environments, cultures, languages, history, and even into the distant future. Through a whirlwind tour of the most influential and important anthropologists and ideas, this book invites you to reconsider your understanding of the world and your place within it.

WHAT IS
ANTHROPOLOGY?

The word "anthropology" comes from the Greek *ánthrōpos*, meaning human being, and *logia*, meaning study. Put simply, it is the study of human beings. But how is this different from other disciplines that focus on humanity, such as philosophy, history, or sociology? The marker that distinguishes anthropology is its combination of multiple perspectives, spanning the natural sciences, social sciences, and humanities. This chapter introduces the origin of the four main subfields and how the first scholars contributed to the subject as it is understood today. You will discover the key schools of thought and the theories that have been dismissed as the discipline evolved. The most popular research methods are outlined, as well as the ethical considerations that anthropologists make when studying and applying their findings. By the end of this chapter, you should have a better idea of what anthropology is, and how it applies to life today.

The history of anthropology

The first anthropological studies are often attributed to Herodotus, a fifth-century Greek historian who wrote about the different cultures and lifestyles of people he encountered while sailing the Mediterranean. His nine scrolls, known as *The Histories*, were unique in observing peoples' commonalities and differences. The later works of scholars such as Ibn Khaldun (1332–1406) and Ibn Battuta (1304–1368/69)—dubbed "the Islamic Marco Polo"—in the fourteenth century first recognized concepts that characterize modern anthropology, such as cultural sensitivity and historical context.

The period between the fifteenth and eighteenth centuries is (controversially) known as the "Age of Discovery," when European explorers travelled across Africa, Asia and the Americas, and encountered previously unknown cultures and languages. Widespread exploitation, violence, slavery, and colonization ensued, justified partly by the anthropological practice at the time. This depicted indigenous people and people from Eastern countries in a demeaning way, as "exotic" or "savages"— essentially, backward to the "civilized" Europeans.

During this period, European anthropologists' curiosity about human diversity was often driven by notions of superiority.

By the nineteenth century, European and American anthropology (which was an established academic discipline by this stage) was focused on considering the similarities and differences between societies, cultures, and physical features of people in the Western world versus those in the Americas, Africa, the Middle East, and Asia. The dominant idea then was that societies passed through a single evolutionary timeline, from "primitive" to the most "advanced"—the latter being Western cultures. This "othering," known as ethnocentrism, continues to haunt the reputation of anthropology in the twenty-first century.

ETHNOCENTRISM

If you use your own culture as a frame of reference for judging another culture (rather than seeing it on its own terms, without judgement), then you are being ethnocentric. In everyday conversations, this can mean that someone is making a culturally biased judgement.

Charles Darwin (1809–1882)

The great advances that anthropology made in the late nineteenth century were largely due to the work of one scientist: Charles Darwin. Contrary to common belief, he did not invent the idea of evolution, as change over time was evident in fossil records in the early nineteenth century. Darwin was, however, the first to figure out the *mechanism* by which evolution works, which is **natural selection**. He proposed that a species' ability to adapt to its surroundings and "fit" into its environment determined its survival. In *The Descent of Man*, published in 1871, Darwin cemented the idea that humans are animals which evolved just like every other organism on Earth. He thought that humans and apes shared a common ancestor in the geological past and predicted, correctly, that because African great apes are most similar to humans, our ancestors evolved first in Africa.

The same but different

During the nineteenth and early twentieth centuries, anthropology was approached from two main perspectives, both greatly influenced by colonialism. The most common was known as "evolutionism," which applied Darwin's evolutionary theory and viewed groups of humans as "social organisms" in a similar fashion to biological organisms. Anthropologists such as Marcel Mauss (1872–1950) and Émile Durkheim (1858–1917) called these groups "societies" and analyzed them as common structures, but with variations between them. The idea was that Western societies had progressed to a state of advanced "civilization" that non-Western societies were aspiring to but had so far not achieved. The alternative approach was "diffusionism," which analyzed common ideas and customs in different cultures through the notion of "culture circles" in which people were generally uninventive and adopted practices from other societies. British anthropologists like W. J. Perry (1887–1949) believed that all cultures originated from a single culture circle in Egypt. Others believed that diffusion occurred from several cultural centers. As the distinct field of anthropology emerged, the hierarchical notions of both theories faced increasing criticism.

Franz Boas (1858–1942)

Known as the "father of American anthropology," Franz Boas rejected the evolutionism practice of comparing cultures to European traditions and the "nomothetic" approach of trying to make generalizations across several cultures at the same time. Instead, Boas argued that each culture should be studied on its own terms. He urged anthropologists to pursue **historical particularism**, which took into account the development and uniqueness of each society. Boas is also known for introducing the theory of **cultural relativism**, which argues that a person's beliefs and behaviors can only be understood in the context of their culture. While observing the Inuit people of Baffin Island in Northern Canada, Boas wrote: "The more I see of their customs, the more I realize that we have no right to look down on them. Where amongst our people would you find such true hospitality? [. . .] We 'highly educated people' are much worse, relatively speaking."

Beyond museums

The work of Franz Boas created a new model for anthropology: while in the US it was previously confined to museums, Boas developed it into an academic discipline. Since then, anthropology became an umbrella term that brought within it four subfields: archaeology, linguistic anthropology, physical anthropology, and cultural anthropology (easily remembered as "stones, tones, bones, and thrones"). Boas believed that this sort of four-field analysis was necessary for achieving an accurate and comprehensive explanation of any anthropological issue. These subcategories can be treated as entirely separate disciplines (this is often the case for European anthropologists), or form part of a holistic approach (such as in the US). The concept of cultural relativism also influenced anthropological research methods. Boas was a strong proponent of living in societies for long periods of time (known as **fieldwork**) to increase understanding and to improve descriptions of those societies. Boas's own fieldwork informed his views and rejection of ethnocentrism.

The main branches of anthropology

🐒 **Biological/physical anthropology** is the study of humans as a biological species. This includes looking at how humans evolved over millions of years, the related species that lived alongside us (which became extinct) and how we interact with other animals. Some biological anthropologists focus on our evolutionary process and consider how modern humans spread throughout the world. Others study humans living today and their physical diversity, such as body size and skin color.

🐒 **Social/cultural anthropology** looks at human social relationships. This includes the ideas and practices that determine all the different ways in which humans classify each other, as well as the roles or expectations that are commonly assigned to them. Psychological anthropology also falls under this subfield, and looks at the interaction between culture and the mind: how human mental health, knowledge, understanding, emotion, and so on are shaped by culture (and vice versa).

- **Linguistic anthropology** is the study of human communication, including spoken language, as well as body language and symbolism.

- **Archaeology** is focused on excavating and analyzing the material products (known as artifacts) of past human life, such as tools, art, and bones, including those from the earliest human societies.

The four-field approach to anthropology strives for a holistic understanding of human behavior. Though anthropologists usually specialize in one of the four subfields, they remain committed to this outlook. By merging areas of expertise, an anthropologist can see the "whole picture" rather than just sections of it. Expertise from other fields—particularly psychology, sociology, and economics—can also help to understand the behavior of people across societies.

Applied anthropology has come to be considered a fifth subfield. It uses the theory and practices of anthropology (from the other subfields) to tackle modern problems, whether through action, policies, or legal changes. For instance, many cultural anthropologists have assisted in the planning of government policies that take account of varied cultural beliefs and needs.

Functionalism

Several theories have dominated anthropology (alongside other disciplines) over the years. The first paradigm that replaced the evolutionary theories of society was functionalism, inspired by the fieldwork of Franz Boas and, most famously, Bronisław Malinowski (1884–1942). This theory was developed following Malinowski's detailed observations and theoretical analyses of the lives of the indigenous islanders in the Trobriand Islands, as set out in his book *Argonauts of the Western Pacific* (1922). Functionalism argues that aspects of culture or social life—such as religion, political arrangements, or kinship—are created to fulfil the basic needs of individuals and hold a function within the overall structure. So, if anthropologists wanted to understand the meaning of something, they simply had to find out what it was *doing*. In this way, functionalists compared societies with biological organisms: just like a living body, a society is made up of different parts that are interrelated, each with its specific functions to be performed. This was the first theory that enabled societies to be compared without moral judgement.

Structural functionalism

Structural functionalism was a form of functionalism that became very popular among social/cultural anthropologists in the UK. It was concerned with the function of things, as well as the wider structure of a society. The most famous proponent was A. R. Radcliffe-Brown (1881–1955), who focused on the system of relationships and institutions that maintained societies (economic, political, religious, and social) and ensured their stability. The functionalist (and structural functionalist) scholars came to be criticized for their disregard of historical processes and change.

DIFFERENT STRUCTURES

This school of thought should not be confused with **structuralism**, which instead focuses on the patterns and rules that form social structures of language, culture, power, and psyche. Three of the most prominent structural anthropologists are Claude Lévi-Strauss (1908–2009), Rodney Needham (1923–2006), and Edmund Leach (1910–1989).

Culture and personality school

The anthropologists Ruth Benedict (1887–1948) and Margaret Mead (1901–1978) pioneered the idea that various aspects of culture shape the personality of individuals within a given society—and personality, once developed, could in turn influence the wider culture. Proponents of this theory argued that the differences between people in various societies usually stemmed from cultural practices instilled early in life. In other words, the foundations of personality development are set in childhood experiences, according to each society's unique cultural traits. In 1928, Margaret Mead's research into the people of Samoa and New Guinea culminated in the publication of *Coming of Age in Samoa*, which concluded that the development of an individual depends on cultural expectations rather than biological traits. By analyzing the behaviors of different genders within the Arapesh, Mundugumor, and Tchambuli tribes, Mead also argued that gender traits are culturally determined. Culture and personality theory was extremely influential from the 1920s to the 1950s and the process of how children learn their culture continues to be of interest to anthropologists.

Cultural ecology and cultural materialism

Cultural ecology (or ecological anthropology) is a term coined by Julian Steward (1902–1972) and considers how cultural adaptations to the natural environment initiate social change and determine social systems. Natural conditions, such as rain, temperature or soil, impact technology, social organization, and attitudes. This approach proposes that the environment influences human adaptation, though does not determine it.

One of the major anthropological perspectives incorporates ideas from cultural ecology and is known as **cultural materialism**. This theory was first proposed by the American anthropologist Marvin Harris (1927–2001) and contends that the material (tangible) aspects of life shape culture. Expanding upon the Marxist concept of historical materialism, Harris said that all behavior can be explained through infrastructure and the economic organization of societies rather than ideas and beliefs, and that anything *useful* to a society will persist. For instance, he argued that cows are sacred in Hinduism because they have greater value alive, by helping farmers to feed their communities, and the food we consume does not have to be shared with them.

An evolving discipline

The symbolic and interpretive anthropology of the 1960s criticized materialist methods of analyzing culture, and instead focused on the study of cultural symbols and rituals. The anthropologist Clifford Geertz (1926–2006) was a famous contributor to this theory, which proposed that symbols help us to gain a better understanding of societies. These ideas changed the direction of anthropology toward issues of culture and interpretation rather than grand narratives of social, political, and economic change. Although it means different things in different disciplines, **postmodernism** came to influence anthropology in the 1980s. Proponents argued that previous theories (particularly in cultural and linguistic anthropology) were biased and lacked objectivity.

Modern-day anthropologists are addressing the discipline's problematic history by adopting practices that recognize bias and promote understanding. In November 2021, the president of the American Anthropological Association issued an apology for "the traumatic effects of anthropology's enduring legacy on Indigenous communities."

Fieldwork and ethnography

A unique feature of anthropology, compared to other social sciences, is its emphasis on ethnographic fieldwork. Unlike the "armchair anthropology" of the eighteenth and nineteenth centuries (whereby data was collected from a distance), fieldwork has been, for the last hundred years, the principal method by which anthropologists gather data, and they have been encouraged to interact and live among societies for extended periods of time. Some anthropologists have taken this a step further, with an activist approach to their research (known as **activist anthropology**). For instance, the anthropologist Charles Hale (b. 1957) worked with the Awas Tingni people of Nicaragua to protect their ancestral lands and provided expert testimony to support their case in court.

LIVING WITH THE INUIT

The British anthropologist Hugh Brody (b. 1943) lived among the Inuit of Northern Canada to learn their native language, *Inuktitut* (which literally means "like an Inuk"). The process involved joining in with many Inuit activities, including hunting trips and fishing expeditions.

THE HUMAN
BODY AND BRAIN

If you want to study human beings, it makes sense to begin your journey through anthropology with an overview of the human body: the key identifier that distinguishes us from all other species on Earth. Through a timeline that spans millions of years, this chapter provides a summary of human evolution, explores the biological history of humans, and creates a context for understanding their physical form and diversity today. As anthropologists' understanding of human evolution is continually developing, this chapter looks at the current evidence about how modern-day *Homo sapiens* developed.

Astonishing discoveries have been made in the twenty-first century regarding the multiple species that lived alongside us, questioning our assumptions about what it means to be human and reminding us of the mysteries that still abound in this discipline. Special attention is paid to the most complex object in the known universe—the human brain. You will see how anthropology has continually tried to understand the differences, while increasingly discovering similarities, between ourselves and the rest of the animal kingdom.

Timeline

(MYA = million years ago, YA = years ago)

TIME	EVENT
55 MYA	First primitive primates evolve.
8–6 MYA	First gorillas evolve. Chimp and human lineages gradually diverge.
6 MYA	*Orrorin tugenensis*, oldest human ancestor likely to have walked on two legs (bipedalism).
5.6 MYA	*Ardipithecus*, the first forest-dwelling bipedal apes appear.
5–2 MYA	*Australopithecines*, referred to as "man-apes," exist. Brains the size of a chimpanzee's, but increasingly bipedal.
3.2 MYA	Lucy, famous specimen of *Australopithecus afarensis* (a species of *Australopithecines*), lives near what is now Hadar, Ethiopia.
2.5 MYA	The Palaeolithic/Old Stone Age period begins. Brain expansion at this stage. Stone tools start to be created by splitting pebbles. Some hominids develop meat-rich diets, possibly causing the evolution of larger brains.

TIME	EVENT
2 MYA	Humanlike hominins appear (*Homo erectus*, also referred to as *Homo ergaster*).
2–1.5 MYA	*Homo erectus* migrate out of Africa in large numbers (to Asia and later Europe); first hunter-gatherer ancestor and use of fire.
600,000–200,000 YA	*Homo heidelbergensis* lives in Africa and Europe (and possibly Asia); similar brain capacity to modern humans.
200,000 YA	*Homo sapiens* (anatomically like modern humans) appear in East Africa. Genetically, we can all trace our lineage back to this small group of humans—separated by approximately 6,666 generations.
150,000 YA	Possibly capable of speech; 100,000-year-old shell jewellery suggests the development of complex speech and symbolism.
117,000 YA	*Homo erectus* die out.
100,000 YA	*Homo sapiens* start migrating out of Africa; exchange of genes with other human species already present in Europe and Asia.

TIME	EVENT
65,000–50,000 YA	"Great leap forward" in several locations around the world; designing decorative jewellery and musical instruments; new weapons and hunting technology invented; cave walls adorned with art and figurative sculptures created—all requiring skill, foresight and abstract thinking.
12,000 YA	Agriculture develops and spreads; first villages.
6,000–5,000 YA	The Sumerians of Mesopotamia develop the world's first civilization.
5,500 YA	Stone Age ends and Bronze Age begins. Humans start to smelt and work copper and tin, and use them instead of stone implements.
5,500 YA	Earliest known writing.

A common ancestor

In the eighteenth century, the scientist Carl Linnaeus developed a system of classifying species that identified three kingdoms of nature (mineral, vegetable, and animal). He was the first to include humans within the animal kingdom, defining us as *Homo sapiens* and primates. We know today that we are related to other types of humans that no longer exist (extinct hominins), as well as ape-like primates, with whom we have always shared the Earth. The exact nature of the evolutionary relationship has not yet been established. A "common ancestor" probably existed 6-8 million years ago but is yet to be identified. Experts believe that a full chronological series of species leading to *Homo sapiens* is impossible.

HOMININI

Zoologists refer to the human tribe as Hominini. We, as *Homo sapiens*, are the only living species remaining but we were likely preceded for millions of years by other hominins and we lived alongside them for some time.

Importance of fossils

In 1924, among the debris at a quarry in South Africa, miners found the fossilized skull of a child with humanlike and ape-like features. Viewed as the "missing link" in the human evolutionary story, this was the first of many discoveries that have confirmed Africa as our place of origin. Fossils continue to be the main way for anthropologists to learn about early humans, though their usefulness is complicated by their limited number and tendency to be in fragments. Through refined excavation methods and records, geochemical dating techniques, and data from other specialized fields, such as genetics and ecology, anthropologists can describe the nature and age of specific fossil specimens and species. However, there is limited scope for fossils to show *how* species lived and *why* they might have either died out or evolved into other species; questions such as these can only be addressed by anthropologists formulating (scientifically informed) scenarios. Ancient DNA can also be recovered from old biological material, such as mummified tissues or ice cores, allowing genetic code to be analyzed.

Our genetic code

When researchers sequenced the chimp genome in 2005, they discovered that we share about 98 percent of our DNA with chimpanzees, making them our closest living relatives. But how, and why, are our skills and abilities so different? The answer, according to biological anthropologists, is a balance between genes (sections of DNA) and environment.

- **Genotype** is an individual's collection of genes inherited from their parents, and passed on to their children (i.e. they are heritable). These determine physical characteristics.

- **Phenotype** refers to the observable physical characteristics, such as height and blood type. These are determined by a person's genotype in combination with environmental factors.

The fundamental difference between our genes and those of chimpanzees lies in the *order* in which the genes are strung on chromosomes (which are basically strands of DNA). Some regions of DNA can trigger activity in other parts of our genes—these regions, which affect our phenotype potential, also vary between humans and chimpanzees.

Two legs

The advent of hominins was probably marked by the development of **bipedalism**—the ability to walk on two legs—with the modern form of walking only evident from the time of *Homo ergaster* (about 2 million years ago). Given the role of both genes and environment for human evolution, this leap in our development from ape-like hominins to the more humanlike abilities and appearance of *Homo ergaster* seems to have been prompted by environmental change: a drop in temperatures across Africa and the creation of wide-open grasslands (known as the savannah). By comparison, those ape-like hominins (which are the ancestors of modern-day chimpanzees) who did not evolve to be bipedal continued to dwell in large forest areas.

ADAPTATION

Adaptation means a variation that increases an organism's biological fitness in a specific environment. Our ability to adapt (e.g. by populating almost the entire globe, across a huge range of environments) is unmatched by other organisms on Earth.

Brain growth

The pioneering ability to stand on two legs (about 2 million years ago) gave us unparalleled advantages over other species. One possible cause of this adaptation was the lack of shade in the savannah; by standing, less surface area was exposed to sunlight and that allowed us to forage during the hottest parts of the day, without danger from predators. This ability also freed up our hands for other tasks, like butchering meat, and thus enabled us to regularly consume food, in greater quantities and with higher calories—allowing our brains to grow. This in turn led to the use of stone tools, which made us even more effective meat scavengers, thus leading to further calories and brain energy. This pattern of rapid brain growth has been recorded from the time of *Homo erectus* until the modern human brain size of around 1,250 cm^3. Other adaptations that propelled our evolution include the pigmentation of our skin, to protect us from the sun's UV-rays, and our ability to cool down through sweating.

Brain size

Anthropologists agree that the growth in our brain size enabled us to improve our hunting and survival skills in the open grasslands of the savannah. However, an evolutionary mystery persists as to why our brains grew to a size that absorbed 20 percent of our daily calories and yet served no immediate benefits for hunting, defence or mating. It is far bigger than it should be for a primate of our size. From birth to adulthood, its volume triples, whereas primate brains only double in size. The exact reason is still a matter of speculation, but many anthropologists believe that larger brains were needed for managing complex relationships in large social groups. Some posit on hominins' improved diet that included fruit (a more nutrient-dense source of food than foliage), with one argument being that finding and remembering the location of fruit was far more complicated than relying on other food items. Other anthropologists suggest that hominins that accumulated knowledge and taught it to others (such as the ability to cook) were more likely to reproduce.

Different Homo species

Homo sapiens began encountering other human species after migrating out of Africa approximately 100,000 years ago. Neanderthals, an advanced species of hominin, lived in Europe and Asia between 400,000 and 30,000 years ago. Asia was also home to *Homo erectus* and *Homo floresiensis*. The location, dispersal, and migration methods of different hominins are still debated, but at least 21 species have been recognized. The popular **"Out of Africa"** hypothesis argues that the modern anatomy of *Homo sapiens* evolved in Africa, and migration caused little to no interbreeding with others. The **multiregional evolution theory** suggests that *Homo sapiens* evolved from earlier hominin species that left Africa first, and that breeding between species was common.

NEANDERTHALS

Neanderthals still exist in the genes of many humans; people of African descent have close to 0.5 percent Neanderthal DNA in their genome, while people of European and Asian descent have roughly 1.7 and 1.8 percent, respectively.

Variation

A unique characteristic of *Homo sapiens* is the diversity in height and body mass, and this variation started early in human evolution. By measuring and comparing fossil fragments in various locations, dating from 1.5–2.5 million years ago, anthropologists have gleaned that some hominins, such as those who lived in South African caves, averaged 4.8 feet tall, while those living in Kenya's Koobi Fora region were almost 6 feet tall. This is because there were selective advantages to being either large or small. For instance, a larger body size was usually associated with greater protection against predators, but it also incurred higher metabolic needs. Since migrating out of Africa, we gradually acclimatized to almost every environment on the planet, resulting in the development of a huge array of physical adaptations, languages, and cultures. Unfortunately, these variations have been used to divide people and instigate wars for thousands of years. The idea of categorizing humans into "races" is an artificial system of classification, without biological foundation. Anthropologists have found that "racial" groups do not hold unique genetic traits.

The cradle of civilization

It is generally agreed that "civilization" refers to a complex human society, relating to the Latin word *civitas* (city). Civilizations first appeared in Mesopotamia (what is now Iraq, and parts of Kuwait, Iran, Syria, and Turkey) and later in Egypt. Mesopotamia's name comes from the Ancient Greek word for "the land between the rivers," a reference to the dry territory between the Tigris and Euphrates rivers, which enabled the start of an agricultural revolution that began almost 12,000 years ago. Several innovations arose from its earliest societies which significantly contributed to human culture and progress, including writing, literature, mathematics, science, law, astronomy, and geometry.

A GIFT FROM THE GODS

The oldest known recipe for beer (or ale) comes from a Mesopotamian poem titled *Hymn to Ninkasi* (c. 1800 BCE)—Ninkasi was the name for the goddess of beer and alcohol. Beer was a daily staple, consumed through a straw to filter out pieces of bread or herbs in the drink.

CULTURE

Why are people different from one another? According to anthropologists, the answer lies in our learned behavior rather than biological differences. For instance, you will automatically move your hand away if you accidentally touch something hot, but any accompanying expletive you say is cultural. While culture does not determine who you are, it is a critical factor that influences your character, behavior, beliefs, diet, and daily life. The question then remains as to why there are so many different cultures.

This chapter challenges you to consider any assumptions you might have about your own culture, and invites you to reflect on how other people grow up and understand the world. Could your behavior or habits seem unusual, inappropriate, or irrational to people from other cultures? By recognizing the ways in which culture affects how we live, cultural anthropology serves to increase our appreciation for the richness and variety of human society today.

What is culture?

The anthropological meaning of the word "culture" is often understood through Edward Burnett Tylor's definition in 1871, as: "that complex whole which includes knowledge, belief, art, morals, law, custom, and any other capabilities and habits acquired by man as a member of society." A cognitive definition of culture was developed in the 1950s, which limited it to the communicative and meaningful aspects of social life: from language to the meaning carried by symbols, persons, actions, and events. This latter concept of culture has been criticized by American cultural anthropology (less so in Europe, where there is a sociological bias). In the 1980s, postmodernists argued that societies are not static units, and some saw culture as a politically dangerous term that might legitimize nationalism and racism. Other anthropologists have argued that the term should no longer be used in the discipline. This debate is reflective of culture's place in anthropology; it is a foundational concept tied to its entire history, and its attempts to define civilization, the nation state, economy, politics, and everyday life across societies.

Researching culture

Cultural anthropology is distinguished by its many and varied research methods, as follows.

 Ethnography is a written description of a society. The cultural anthropologist who writes it (also known as an ethnographer) gathers as much information as possible, from many angles, to gain a holistic view of a culture.

Participant observation involves living within a community and participating in daily activities. Pioneered by Bronisław Malinowski, this process involves more than simply talking to people. It includes one-on-one interviews with cultural experts, focus groups, questionnaires, and surveys.

 An **informant** is usually someone with a lot of knowledge about the group being studied. They are interviewed and used as a contact point with the group.

The **genealogical method** entails learning the kinship, family, and marriage patterns of a group.

 Life histories uncover the personal backgrounds of individuals. This approach can help anthropologists to arrive at some insights into perceptions about a culture.

- 🐒 **Interpretive anthropology** requires the ethnographer to reflect on the impact that their presence has on the study group and how their personal culture influences the interpretation of what they observe. This approach developed in the 1970s, with greater awareness of the researcher's ethnocentrism and the need to understand the natives' viewpoint. Interpretive anthropology was a response to early ethnographies that attempted to portray a scientific, objective view of society (known as **ethnographic realism**).

- 🐒 In **problem-oriented ethnography**, data is collected exclusively on a specific research question while in the field.

- 🐒 **Ethnohistory** involves the reconstruction of the history of a society using library and archival research, including accounts from members of that society and outside observers.

- 🐒 In **ethnology**, cross-cultural comparison and analysis is employed to understand the similarities and differences among cultures. This can help anthropologists to understand the processes of change and adaptation within societies.

Up, down and sideways

Until the 1970s, cultural anthropology was mainly a Western-based discipline, with most fieldwork conducted in Africa, Asia, the Middle East, Latin America, the Pacific Islands, and with Native American populations in the US; it was their "difference" that fascinated Western anthropologists. The focus was on smaller, non-literate societies, regular people and others who had rarely been objects of scientific study, including families and local communities (rather than populations on a larger scale, royalty or those in power). In 1972, Laura Nader challenged anthropologists to think more broadly and to "study up, down and sideways." Since then, anthropology has become more global in scope, and now every individual and society are of interest and considered part of the continuum of human culture.

SOCIETY AND CULTURE—WHAT'S THE DIFFERENCE?

Society refers to a group of people who live within some type of bordered area and who share a common way of life. Culture is the common way of life within the society.

Are you cultured?

When a person is described as "cultured," the term refers to the word's origin, from the German *Kultur*, meaning civilization; to be "cultured" is to be civilized, educated, and sophisticated. From anthropology's perspective, we are *all* "cultured," because culture is all-encompassing; it relates to all the material objects, behaviors, and activities of people, as well as their values and beliefs. The capacity for culture is universal, but it evolves differently within each society. Social interaction exposes individuals to local cultural traditions through observation, teaching, reward, or punishment. This process of learning the rules and values of a culture is known as **enculturation** and starts in childhood.

PARENTING

Children's interaction with their parents often acts as the archetype of how to behave around others—including expectations and taboos. For instance, in comparing conversation styles, American and European children tend to be self-focused, expressing personal preferences, and challenging authority, while Korean and Chinese children speak briefly and describe themselves in relation to others.

Cultural variation

Culture manifests itself in how we think and communicate. Even time can be viewed differently, according to symbols and customs particular to a given culture. In Chinese culture, each year is marked by one of 12 signs associated with a particular animal, in an aspect of yin or yang. There are varied norms regarding lateness; arriving too late is one of the top ten topics people dream about in Germany (this is often an unconscious sign of anxiety), whereas late starts and endings to meetings are common in Turkey. A distinction is often made between "clock time" and "event time" cultures. People living in the former tend to schedule their lives by the clock and time is considered a fixed rule (e.g. lunch is at 12 o'clock). Broadly speaking, Western countries and Japan run on "clock time." In "event time" cultures, social events determine the start, duration and end of activities (e.g. when friends meet, they will eat lunch). Event time was standard in human history, and still dominates in India and the Islamic world.

Two aspects of communication are often cited as demonstrating cultural differences: insult and humour. The psychologist Saba Safdar argues that common insults

in a culture show the important values within a group, because they deny such values and strip the person of that characteristic. In individualist cultures, where people are independent and self-contained, insults are usually personal and directed toward the target's psychological or physical characteristics (e.g. idiot, ugly, rude, etc.). In collectivist cultures, where the group is paramount, insults tend to be relational (e.g. your mother is a . . .).

JOKES ACROSS CULTURES

Some form of shared knowledge is said to be key for humour. For instance, quotes from the TV show *Seinfeld* create affiliation for many North American people. One study found that Americans are more likely to tell sex jokes than Singaporeans, a reflection of broad cultural norms; Singapore is a more conservative society, with pornography banned by law. Singaporeans preferred violent or aggressive jokes, which researchers linked to the country's competitive culture.

Cultural change

All cultures around the world are resistant to change but it is an unavoidable reality, particularly when there is contact between societies (e.g. through globalization and the internet) or environmental factors at play (e.g. climate change). Invention, whether technological or ideological, can lead to cultural change. An example is the "streaming revolution" in the twenty-first century, which changed viewers' habits, blurred the lines between television and film, and reduced the number of people visiting movie theatres. Changes in transport methods in the coming decades, such as increased use of electric cars or more bicycle lanes in cities, will inevitably impact cultures around the world.

CULTURE LOSS

Acculturation is what happens when one culture comes to dominate another and substantially replaces traditional cultural patterns. An example of this is Native American culture, which has been largely acculturated after centuries of pressure from European Americans to adopt their ways. The majority of Native Americans now speak English instead of their ancestral language.

Material culture tends to diffuse faster than non-material culture (known as **culture lag**). A new piece of technology can spread through society in a matter of months, but it takes longer for cultural acceptance of it. For instance, the invention of cars required roads and petrol stations to be built, new laws to be passed, and so forth.

Alternatively, at an individual level, a person can move to another society and adopt its culture. This is known as **transculturation** and can be seen when immigrants learn the language of their new country and adopt its cultural patterns.

GREETINGS DURING A PANDEMIC

During the Covid-19 pandemic, greetings altered to reflect cultural differences. In France, cheek kisses were replaced by a verbal exchange of "*Bisous!*" In Tanzania, formal bows to elders, as well as long handshakes and kisses between peers, were substituted by distanced bowing and foot shakes. In the United Arab Emirates, traditional nose kisses were swapped with waving or placing a hand on the heart.

Survivals

In anthropological discussions of cultural change or stability, one term you might come across is "survivals." This was first coined by Edward Burnett Tylor in 1871 and refers to cultural phenomena that have outlived their original practical function and yet continue to exist. They were previously known as "superstitions." As the sociologist Margaret Hodgen wrote in 1931, these resilient customs, ideas and opinions had a logical place in history but now remain as "illogical and inharmonious misfits" within a culture.

TIES AND TAILCOATS

In medieval Europe, a leather tie was once an emblem of being a knight, which denoted wealth, strength, and virility. This symbol remained but the fabric changed over time, from leather to silk and cotton. Tailcoats (or dress coats) evolved from clothes designed in the eighteenth century for convenient horse riding, hence the waist-length front and split back.

Celebrity culture

As with all kinds of culture, "celebrity culture" can be difficult to define but it is a term you may be familiar with. It refers to a society's preoccupation with famous individuals, and an excessive interest in their personal lives. The study of celebrity and public personas has steadily increased within anthropology, with research focusing on its significance and meaning within different societies. Jamie Tehrani asserts that celebrity culture is rooted in basic human instincts that were once crucial to human survival. Unlike other primates, whose social hierarchy is based on dominance, humans respect or admire members of their community—a characteristic known as **prestige**. This was once bestowed on individuals who had superior skills or knowledge (e.g. an excellent hunter or toolmaker) that allowed new discoveries and inventions to spread across communities. This makes us focus on successful role models and feel inclined to copy their behavior, because our brains are programmed to attach prestige to the individual generally, rather than to specific traits that they display. Fame has become "the primary cue of prestige."

IDENTITY AND
PERSONHOOD

What are you? From a biological perspective, you are of course a human being. But the idea of being a "person" is something different, and that is subject to a variety of interpretations. Defining personhood differs between cultures around the world and essentially rests on identifying four indicators: the beginning of personhood, what it means to be a person, how it may change and when (or indeed, whether) it ends. Philosophy, psychology, religion, history, and even local laws have a part to play in shaping how personhood is defined. This chapter looks at the differences that anthropologists have identified in the ways in which personhood, self, and identity are constructed within different cultures, as well as the numerous ways that a person's place can be defined within wider society. This includes a look at rites of passage and coming-of-age markers, as well as the importance of language in shaping ideas of personhood.

What is personhood?

Personhood is a term used by anthropologists to indicate who, within any given culture, is considered a fully functioning and accepted member of society. The cross-cultural study of personhood is filled with debate because the terms "person" and "self" are not always clearly defined. Beliefs about what it is to be a person can include notions of "self," which is usually associated with introspection and the psychological entity, such as an ego or a person's subjective experience of being. Some anthropologists, such as Sarah Lamb and Sarah Rasmussen, prefer to use the broader, more objective term "person." In India, for example, Nandita Chaudhary's research found that there are multiple definitions of "self," depending on the situation; it is meaningful when applied to spiritual/religious contemplation but in other contexts, the "self" without reference to an individual's family is an "incomplete" phenomenon. The task of anthropologists studying personhood within any given society is to discover what defines being a person, or being human, without being influenced by their own personal cultural assumptions about the meaning of these concepts.

The beginning of personhood

One of the issues that distinguishes cultural ideas of personhood is the point in time when an embryo, fetus or newborn baby is thought to become a person. This remains a controversial topic, given stormy public debates about the legality of abortion, the inclusion of fetal tissue in medicine and the use of life support machines for extremely premature infants. Different religions propose ideas about the start of personhood: Roman Catholicism, for example, teaches that human life begins at the moment of conception, whereas Hinduism contains the idea of reincarnation, so there is no clear beginning or end to personhood. In several countries, a naming ceremony or a formal birth registration process provides a new human being with the legal status of being a person, at which moment they gain the associated rights and entitlements of the society they are born into (such as vaccinations, citizenship or healthcare). In the twenty-first century, the impact of genetic sciences and reproductive technologies has created new ethical and political questions for anthropologists to explore.

The end of personhood

Anthropologists have often considered the distinctions that cultures make between the social and biological death of a person. This includes the practical and ethical questions surrounding euthanasia, suicide, ceremonies, mourning rituals, and how the subject of death is generally addressed (or avoided) in different societies. At the beginning of the twentieth century, the anthropologist Robert Hertz claimed that while a society transcends the lives of its individual members, the death of an individual is a social event and marks the beginning of a ceremonial process by which the deceased becomes an ancestor. Some anthropologists have suggested that the social existence of a dead person can be maintained through attendance and maintenance of their graveside.

THE FUN IN FUNERAL

In New Orleans, USA, jazz funerals have been used since the late 1800s to celebrate the life of a lost community member. A brass band marches from the church to the burial site, followed by the friends and family joining the parade.

Continuity of life

Reincarnation and resurrection—concepts that abound in many cultures around the world—pose a challenge for anthropologists who come from societies that assume a linear path through life, with a clearly marked beginning at birth and end at death. For instance, Buddhism teaches that the actions of a person lead to a new existence after death (known as the rebirth doctrine), in an endless cycle called samsara. Through karma and eventual enlightenment, Buddhists hope to escape samsara and achieve nirvana, an end to suffering. The anthropologist Akhil Gupta has also highlighted that a belief in the continuity of life means that reincarnated children "have to be reconceptualised as more complex beings than is allowed by the standard narrative of childhood." For instance, among the Beng people of Côte d'Ivoire, all babies are said to be a reincarnation of someone who has died, and newborns are often treated in the same way as adults.

Making a person

According to the findings of anthropologists, a person can exist in countless ways, some of which do not even require the physical presence of a body. Exploring a range of beliefs can help to challenge your own cultural perceptions of what constitutes personhood. One perspective that is popular among anthropologists is to look at societies in terms of the roles that people play and the importance of relationships in defining personhood. Within some cultures, persons are defined in relation to their wider community or society. A clear example of this is Japan, where the expression for a fully grown adult literally means "one helping," and people are addressed according to their age and status in society. Among the Zafimaniry people of Madagascar, the point in time when a human being becomes a "person" varies greatly between individuals because it depends on levels of moral responsibility. Birth is not the defining characteristic; instead, personhood is gradually acquired through marriage, child-rearing and the "hardening" of a house to make it durable and weather-proof.

In many societies, newborn babies are not considered persons or fully human, which adds to the idea that

personhood is not a natural or innate quality but is contingent on the cultural context. Some anthropologists focus their research on "social births:" events that mark the entry of a person into society and that are often celebrated by rituals. The notion of "social births" is useful because it reinforces the slow and changeable processes often involved in being recognized as a person. For example, personhood for the Mapuche people of Chile and Argentina is dependent on the relationships that individuals build throughout the course of their lives, and it is not fully achieved until death.

TRANSHUMANISM

Transhumanists argue that science and technology will enable humanity to overcome its biological limitations, both mental and physical, and create a radically enhanced post-human species and society. How will personhood be defined in an age of cyborg technology, artificial worlds and enhanced human abilities?

Rites of passage

When somebody undergoes a significant change in life, cultures around the world often mark it with a "rite of passage," meaning a ritual that provides the person with a new status. They are also sometimes known as coming-of-age ceremonies. In the twentieth century, the anthropologist Victor Turner identified three stages commonly found in these rituals around the world.

1. **Separation** is when a person withdraws from a group (physically or mentally).

2. **Liminality** refers to the "betwixt and between" stage, when a person exists in limbo between two stages.

3. **Reintegration** involves the person returning to their group, having been transformed by the experience, and with a new outlook and sense of purpose.

Many rites of passage are based in religion. For instance, Jewish boys and girls celebrate their Bar and Bat Mitzvahs at age 13 and 12 respectively to demonstrate their commitment to their faith. When Muslim girls in Malaysia

turn 11, they attend a prestigious ceremony called Khatam Al Koran that demonstrates their growing maturity.

Notable events in a person's life—particularly those surrounding birth, marriage, retirement and death—are acknowledged in almost all cultures to be important rites of passage. However, the way in which these occasions are recognized varies considerably across countries and regions, and within different religious and ethnic groups. For instance, the passage from girlhood to womanhood is marked in Spanish-speaking countries through a quinceañera (a special religious mass followed by an elaborate *fiesta*) and in Amish communities through unsupervised weekends away from home.

A COW AND A BACHELOR PARTY

The Hamer people of the Omo valley in Ethiopia have a tradition requiring grooms-to-be to successfully jump a (castrated) male cow four times, while naked, before they can marry. If they are successful, they earn the title of "Maza" and are deemed ready to wed. During this ceremony, Hamer women are voluntarily whipped to show their loyalty to the groom-to-be.

Me or we?

The culture you grow up in plays a large role in determining how you see yourself in relation to society. Some cultures are individualistic (or "me" societies), such as Australia, North America and northern parts of Europe. Individuals are generally deemed responsible for their own wellbeing and that of their immediate family members only. Comparatively, collectivist societies (or "we" cultures)—of which China, Mexico and Turkey are examples—prioritize strong social ties and belonging to a large group. The individual in such a society is more likely to base decisions on the wellbeing of their group rather than their personal needs or desires.

THE ORIGINAL AFFLUENT SOCIETY

Until the 1960s, the Ju/'hoansi "bushmen" of Namibia were an egalitarian society. Anthropologist James Suzman noted that hunters who brought back large amounts of meat to feed their group were (jovially) insulted and given the same quantity of food as everybody else, in order to maintain fairness and prevent selfishness. As a 200,000-year-old culture, they were the most successful society in human history.

Western societies tend to value personal success over group achievement, which in turn is also associated with the need for personal choice, greater self-esteem, and the pursuit of individual happiness. Studies show that this often results in people overestimating their abilities. Research into East Asian societies, which are considered to be more collectivist, has found self-inflation to be almost completely absent and that people are more likely to underestimate their abilities.

DIFFERENT WAYS OF SEEING

Research shows that people from collectivist versus individualist cultures tend to analyze images differently. An eye-tracking study by Richard Nisbett found that participants from East Asia tend to be more holistic. They spend more time looking around the background of an image and working out the context of the situation. People in the USA were more inclined to concentrate on the central elements of the picture.

Environmental personhood

For several hundred years, in Europe and its colonies, legal personhood was mostly limited to white, able-bodied, heterosexual, cisgender men. Legal personhood expanded during the twentieth century, alongside the advancement of liberalism and human rights. Since the 1970s, environmental personhood has been posited as a way of protecting nature (natural entities traditionally being legal "objects," lacking rights or powers). In 2014, Te Urewera forest, the ancestral home of the Tūhoe people, was recognized by the New Zealand government as a legal person. Statutory guardians were granted to the forest and land ownership rights were transferred to Te Urewera itself. Adopting indigenous environmentalism into legal frameworks is a growing movement in several countries, such as Ecuador, Bolivia, and India.

"I AM THE RIVER, THE RIVER IS ME"

In Māori culture, ancestors (*tupuna*) live on in nature. It is the community's duty to protect both the landscape they inherit and the people who lived there before them.

COMMUNICATION

Across the world, there are approximately 6,000–7,000 languages—a diversity that reveals an ongoing process of adaptation that continues to this day. All humans share a capacity for communication and many view language as the most important characteristic of culture. Without this ability, the variety and complexity of human cultures would not exist or be sustained throughout the centuries. This chapter looks at the work of linguistic anthropologists, who consider the many ways in which humans communicate, the sounds and function of language, and the impact that different systems of communication have on the lives of individuals and societies. Taking the definition of communication as being "those acts by which one organism triggers another" (Charles Hockett), this overview will include spoken language as well as non-verbal forms, such as body language, symbolism, and appearance. You will be introduced to the ways in which language can inform your world view and political opinions, as well as how speech can be used to express identity.

Language vs communication

Communication, in which all animals engage, is a process for information exchange between individuals through a system of symbols, signs, and/or behaviors. This can include gestures, odours, sounds, or physical movement. These **closed systems** of communication inhibit new meanings and are limited to the present temporal moment. Language is a human form of communication that relies solely on symbols to convey meaning (which can include sounds, words or gestures with an assigned meaning). It is an **open system** of communication because it adapts to environmental and social changes, with new meanings and symbols constantly being created. Language also enables the expression of ideas regarding the past or future.

ALL LANGUAGE IS SYMBOLIC

A symbol is anything that represents something else— something tangible, an idea or an observation. Symbols are **arbitrary**, as there is no obvious connection between them and their meaning, hence, "That which we call a rose by any other name would smell as sweet." (William Shakespeare's *Romeo and Juliet*)

The evolution of language

Anthropologists generally agree that communication among our human ancestors started in the same way as it did for our primate relatives, through a combination of sounds, facial expressions, scent, touch, and body language (otherwise known as **gesture-call** communication). At some point during our evolution, we developed the ability to manipulate our vocal cords, lips, and tongues to produce the human speech and language skills we are familiar with today. Anthropologists have identified three key adaptations to explain this: the human brain, hands, and larynx.

The "seat of speech" in the human brain was first identified by the physician and anthropologist Paul Broca in 1861, as a region that allows the intricate muscle movements of the lungs, larynx, and airways needed for modern human speech production. Damage to this area of the brain can leave a person incapable of communicating with others. Since then, many parts of the brain are now understood to be language-related, which has led anthropologists to believe that language evolved over 2 million years, becoming more elaborate as structures in the brain and throat changed.

Your hands also play an important part in communication. The dexterity of the human hand allows for a huge range of gestures that enable language to be more efficient, as well as the ability to manipulate objects, including instruments for written language (or typing instruments in the modern age). Informal written languages likely developed around 35,000 years ago, through drawings and cave paintings that told stories. Written language, consisting of specific marks in wet clay with a reed implement (known as **cuneiform**), was invented in Mesopotamia around 5,500 years ago. In terms of human speech, the arrangement of airways and larynx (voice box), which modify the airflow from the lungs, enables a huge range of possible sounds. In particular, the low position of the larynx in the throat of humans—evident in *Homo sapiens* from 200,000 years ago—creates the necessary space for more air to travel before it reaches the lips, therefore enabling the variety of complex sounds found in different languages across the world.

Language acquisition

All human infants have an innate faculty for language. Without the need for any formal education or instruction, all children learn language through observing social cues and listening to the words, sounds, and grammatical rules of the people around them. The linguist Noam Chomsky called this ability the **language acquisition device** and argued that the basic template for all language is embedded in our genes—a theory known as **universal grammar**. While this is controversial, common principles and conditions can be seen to feature across all languages.

- **Phonemes** are basic, discrete sounds, such as consonants and vowels.

- **Morphemes** are the combinations of sounds that have meanings, such as words, or sounds in words that indicate gender or plurality.

- **Syntax** is the combination of morphemes and words to form phrases and sentences according to specific patterns and rules (i.e. the rules of word order).

Evidence shows that this ability to naturally learn a language exists until around the age of 12—an idea known as the **critical age range hypothesis**.

Non-verbal communication

The psychologist Albert Mehrabian identified the minor role that words play in direct human communication. In the 1970s, he established the 7-38-55 rule which states that 55 percent of meaning is communicated through body language, 38 percent through facial expression, and 7 percent through spoken word. It is therefore not surprising that linguistic anthropologists have conducted extensive research into the different ways in which cultures communicate through non-verbal means, including the study of body movements and gestures (**kinesics**), social distance and space (**proxemics**), and the rules of physical touch (**haptics**). Paralanguage is also explored, which looks at how words are modified or clarified through pitch and speed of talking, volume, tempo, noises, pauses, or gestures.

There are cultural variations in the way speech volume is interpreted. In Arabic cultures, speaking loudly denotes strength and sincerity, and Germans view it as self-confidence, whereas Filipino and Japanese people associate speaking softly with good manners and self-control.

Function of language

The Afghan-born American novelist Khaled Hosseini once wrote: "If culture was a house, then language was the key to the front door, to all the rooms inside." The critical importance of language is the reason why anthropologists often learn the language of a society to gain a thorough understanding of its culture. This includes the subtleties of non-verbal communication, such as facial expressions and hand gestures, as well as generational differences between age groups (e.g. the words used by teenagers and the elderly). The anthropologist Edward Sapir pointed out that, unlike walking, which is an "instinctive" function within humans, language is a "non-instinctive method of communicating ideas, emotions, and desires by means of a system of voluntarily produced symbols"—a system that varies from one society to another, and that *creates* as much as it *describes* different realities. Vocabulary and language are therefore a very sensitive index of the history and culture of a people.

Why we gossip

Many primates, such as baboons, live in big groups and use grooming as a social tool to make connections, build trust and form alliances. The anthropologist Robin Dunbar has argued that humans developed language to serve the same purpose, but far more efficiently. In particular, our use of language for gossip—defined as talking about people who are not present—is the human equivalent of primate grooming. During our evolutionary history, Dunbar explains, human groups expanded to a size and complexity such that regular grooming became impractical as a social glue. Gossip enabled large groups to stay together and helped our ancestors survive because it allowed valuable information to spread across large networks of friends and family, where personal observations or interactions were not possible. Gossip enabled social norms to be communicated and kept bad behavior in check. Anthropological research also shows that gossip is a cross-cultural phenomenon, which supports the idea of its evolutionary benefits.

Language, thoughts and behavior

Anthropologists Edward Sapir and Benjamin Whorf developed a theory in 1929 suggesting that the structure and words of a language shape the speaker's perception and view of reality. The **Sapir–Whorf hypothesis** (or linguistic relativity hypothesis) offers examples including the 92 words that exist for rice among the Hanunóo people of the Philippines, the over 400 words and expressions for snow in Scotland and the lack of a word meaning "privacy" in Russian. Most cognitive scientists reject this and instead argue that language influences (rather than controls) a speaker's mind, particularly regarding what they habitually think about; so, a language's vocabulary suggests what is, and is not, important and habitually discussed within a culture.

The Australian aboriginal language of *Guugu Yimithirr* has no concept of left/right or forward/backward. Its speakers do not refer to the position of things in relation to themselves, but relative to the cardinal points—north, south, east, and west.

Language travels

The migration of people throughout history has also led to the movement of languages. Language can travel by being imposed on others (as in colonialism), or by serving as a form of solidarity or **ethnic boundary marker** for minority populations (such as in African American Vernacular English). Particular words can also cross borders and be adopted across geographic areas. For instance, English is the primary or official language of 101 countries and its influence spreads further due to many other languages having adopted its words within their vocabulary. This status and reach go back to the British Empire, which governed almost a quarter of the world's population in 1913.

PSEUDO-ANGLICISMS AROUND THE WORLD

Beauty farm—in Italian, meaning a spa.

Skinship—in Korean, it refers to platonic hand-holding or hugging.

Tokbek (talk back)—in Hebrew, meaning a comment on a blog or website.

Dialects and different cultures

Across cultures and geographic locations, the same language can be spoken with a variety of dialects (meaning social or regional variations). The degree of difference usually increases with distance, such as the originary French spoken in France versus its variations in Switzerland, Jersey, Quebec (in Canada) and Lebanon, where one language variety blends with other nearby tongues. However, a "standard" version of most languages is often elevated as the **prestige dialect** and all others are deemed to be subordinate or rural dialects. There is no inherent superiority in this standardized dialect; it just tends to be the type that is spoken by the most socially or politically powerful in a society, or within urban areas (especially capital cities). This is why linguistic anthropologists often say, "A language is a dialect with an army and a navy." (A quote often attributed to Max Weinreich.) For instance, in Thailand, standard Thai is based on the dialect of the educated classes of Bangkok, and native speakers often refer to the regional variants as "different kinds of Thai."

Language and identity

The way you speak can be seen as a marker of certain identities, such as your ethnicity, social class, age, gender, and even your workplace. Speaking in the prestige dialect of a language, like "received pronunciation" in the UK, can indicate a higher level of education or social class. In cultures that contain many dialects and accents, people regularly alter their speaking style, depending on what is appropriate for the situation—a practice called **code switching**. Think about how you speak to friends compared to how you address your employer or when you speak publicly.

FEMALE SPEECH PATTERNS

Studies show that women are more likely to use an upward inflection at the end of sentences, making statements sound like questions (known as **uptalk**), or to drop their pitch at the end of words or sentences (known as **vocal fry** or **creaky voice**). These patterns are often perceived negatively, but linguists say that they demonstrate a speaker's empathy, friendliness, and cooperative manner.

The digital age

The modern age has been marked by mass movements of people, from rural to urban areas and across countries, as well as technological advances that divide populations into **digital natives** (those growing up with digital technologies) and **digital immigrants** (those learning to use them later in life). These developments are leading to a steady decline in the quantity of languages spoken across the world, as well as new forms of electronic communication being created. English has become the global language of business and finance, and North American culture permeates most societies. Linguistic anthropologists predict that 1,500 endangered languages will no longer be spoken by the next century.

EMOJIS

The word emoji is inspired by two Japanese words: "e" for "picture" and "moji" meaning "character." Invented in Japan in the 1990s, they became widely available on mobile computing devices in 2011. Though not a language, emojis are a system of communication that fulfils some of the functions of a language.

RELIGION
AND BELIEF

Whether you are an atheist, agnostic, or staunch believer, there is no denying the huge impact that religion has had on the human species. Its influence is felt in countless ways, both banal and momentous, from the most popular names in a society or people's clothing choices, to the national holidays your country celebrates and conflicts occurring around the world on any given day. As a central part of human history, religion is extremely important to anthropologists. Their focus is not on identifying the best or correct belief system, or discovering truths or falsehoods. Anthropologists are interested in understanding the interplay between religion and culture, as well as how faith and belief systems shape people's perceptions of their place in society and how the universe is organized. This chapter introduces you to the common elements shared across most religions, as well as the meaning of religion, the theories about its purpose in society, and how its impact may change in the years to come.

What is religion?

Defining religion is not as straightforward as it might seem; some anthropologists, like Talal Asad, argue that any definition is inherently problematic due to its cross-cultural application. It should not be too exclusive or broad, historically limited or culturally specific. It is difficult to avoid ethnocentrism and viewing one religion as the archetype. Not all societies have a word for religion, because religious or spiritual practices and routines form such an intrinsic part of everyday life, and these habits are also intertwined with magic in some cultures. The many definitions that exist can, however, be grouped into three categories: **substantive** definitions, which describe the distinctive properties or attributes of religions; **functional** definitions, which focus on the function that religions perform in the lives of individuals and communities; and the **family resemblance** definitions, such as Benson Saler's approach of identifying overlapping similarities and central tendencies. For simplicity, there are four dimensions that seem to be present, in varying forms and intensities, in all types of religion: belief, ritual, spiritual experience, and unique social forms of community.

Religious beliefs

Anthropologists agree that religions characterize humanity's relationship with the supernatural or transcendent world, with the latter meaning something greater than the individual *and* beyond the material world. This is what distinguishes religion from other value or belief systems, such as politics or philosophy. An example of a religious belief is what, or who, is held to be divine.

- **Polytheism** is the worship of multiple gods and is well documented in history (e.g. the Ancient Egyptians, Romans and Greeks). Current examples include Hinduism and Native American folk beliefs.

- **Monotheism** means believing in one invisible entity beyond the natural world; Christians call this "God," Muslims use "Allah," and Jews say "Yahweh."

- **Atheism** means believing in no deities, such as in Buddhism.

- **Animism** is the belief that objects, places, and creatures possess a spiritual essence. Examples include indigenous Philippine folk religions and many indigenous cultures.

Émile Durkheim

Sociologist Émile Durkheim defined religion as "a unified set of beliefs and practices relative to sacred things, that is to say, things set apart and forbidden—beliefs and practices which unite [into] one single moral community called a Church, all those who adhere to them." He argued that all societies divide the world into two categories.

- The **sacred** (holy) is anything that transcends everyday life, typically taking the form of collective or community acts of religious rituals.

- The **profane** (unholy) relates to ordinary life and its mundane, repetitive activities.

In the context of industrialization and escalating suicide rates across late nineteenth century Western Europe, Durkheim claimed that religion was unique in alleviating people's sense of isolation. He presented a groundbreaking "integration theory" claiming that the Catholic Church's integrated structure and sanctions against suicide were deterrents against self-annihilation among its members. In comparison, he argued that religious freedom of thought and lack of integration among members of Protestant denominations explained their higher suicide rates.

Rituals

Anthropologist Victor Turner defined a ritual as "a stereotyped sequence of activities [. . .] performed in a sequestered place, and designed to influence preternatural entities or forces on behalf of the actors' goals and interests." Due to their central role and the continuity they bring across generations of believers, a great deal of anthropological research has focused on identifying and interpreting the rituals practised in a wide variety of religions. As well as the obvious physical gestures or actions that might spring to mind, such as prayers and mantras, rituals also include the way in which religions mark significant life events or identity transitions, such as births, marriages, or deaths. The ethnographer Arnold van Gennep called these **"rites of passage,"** which can be purpose-driven (such as religiously sanctioning a couple's union) or symbolic (such as a white wedding dress to symbolize purity). For instance, the sun dance rituals practised by First Nations communities in Canada celebrate the Earth and sun, and involve participants performing feats of endurance and personal sacrifices on behalf of their community.

From a psychological perspective, rituals can also provide access to "spiritual powers," particularly during times when people face challenges in life. David DeSteno's research has found that many religious rituals impact the way the brain works. For instance, Christians often say grace before a meal and Jews give thanks to God with the *Modeh Ani* prayer every day upon waking; both are acts of gratitude, which is a mindset that can make people more virtuous. The synchronicity within many rituals also helps to build connection within communities; an example of this is the way both Buddhists and Hindus often chant in prayer, and Christians and Muslims regularly kneel and stand during worship. This echoes the findings of anthropologists, showing that rituals can serve to enhance the sense of togetherness among believers. This might explain the continued presence of religion; as DeSteno says: "When it comes to finding ways to help people deal with issues surrounding birth and death, morality and meaning, grief and loss, it would be strange if thousands of years of religious thought didn't have something to offer."

Spiritual experience

Anthropologist Clifford Geertz argued that religions provide members with an ethos and a world view of "reality," so that both the everyday and extraordinary events in people's lives can relate to something transcendent and bigger than themselves. Numerous studies support this, with evidence showing that religious faith can contribute to, and promote, wellbeing, personal security, and social connectedness. For instance, many religions attach spiritual importance to places, such as the place of birth or death of founders or saints, or locations where miracles were performed or witnessed. Religious devotees are encouraged to travel to these places, through a journey known as a **pilgrimage**.

KUMBH MELA

Kumbh Mela is a major pilgrimage and festival in Hinduism. It is one of the largest gatherings of humans in the world, where pilgrims gather to bathe in four riverbank sites. Bathing in the sacred or holy rivers is said to bring *prāyaścitta* (atonement, penance) for past mistakes, and cleanse believers of their sins.

Social forms of community

Beyond the individual, religion can also provide a sense of group identity, enabling people to come together to communicate the same thoughts, or participate in the same actions or **"collective effervescence,"** as Émile Durkheim described it. The sociologists Lorne L. Dawson and Joel Thiessen have identified four key elements regarding the social dimension of religions. First, that beliefs of a religion gain credibility through being shared and agreed upon by a group, which encourages more people to believe. Second, religion provides an authority that deals with life's most vexing questions, such as moral issues or determining the best way to live. The values and ideals of a society often originate in the shared beliefs of a religion. Third, religion helps to shape different aspects of a community and the foundations for self-control, which are vital for any functional society. Fourth, places of religious worship provide social hubs within communities, as possible centers for socializing, entertainment, and support.

Religious practitioners

Religious beliefs are taught to followers by authority figures, through formal doctrines and informally through stories, songs, and myths. There is no universal term for religious practitioners, but most fall under one of three categories. **Priests** are said to be the intermediaries between God (or the gods) and humans, with authority stemming from religious scriptures or qualifications. For instance, Hindu priests, or *pujaris*, must learn Sanskrit and spend years becoming proficient in Hindu ceremonies. **Prophets** claim to have a direct connection to the divine and to be able to communicate divine messages to others. In Christianity, Islam, and Judaism, Moses is a prophet who received direct revelations from God. **Shamans** can communicate with the supernatural, and are summoned to perform special ceremonies and rituals.

In 2000, anthropologist Scott Hutson described similarities between the altered state of consciousness achieved by shamans and the feeling of people dancing in a rave (a large dance party). The DJ at these events is often called a "techno-shaman."

Crisis of faith

Secularization is defined as the process of social change during which a society becomes less religious over time. This can be seen in countries such as Canada, the Czech Republic, Estonia, France, Germany, Japan, the Netherlands, South Korea, the UK, and Uruguay, which have some of the lowest belief rates in the world, despite religion playing a central role in their societies just a century or so ago. The common thread among all these countries is that they provide their citizens with a relatively high level of stability (political and economic, including social security systems) and education. Anthropologists propose that the sense of security that religion can provide is therefore not as appealing or necessary. Some religions have attempted to modernize from within, by updating their beliefs and practices to reflect changes in contemporary culture (known as organizational secularization). While many anthropologists equate secularization with modernization, some find evidence of religious revitalization in the twenty-first century, such as the growth and export of Pentecostalism from the USA.

Religion in the twenty-first century

The decline in religious belief is unlikely to mark the beginning of its disappearance. One reason is that religion seems to give meaning to suffering—much more so than any scientific knowledge or secular ideal that we know of. Research shows that many people in the twenty-first century continue to believe in a greater being or life force guiding the world, or in the efficacy of prayer or other ritual practices, even though they might never attend conventional religious services. The direction of people's beliefs and practices has also changed, with a greater desire for holistic, flexible, "spiritual growth"-oriented types of religious experiences.

MEANING IN SUFFERING

In 2011, a massive earthquake struck Christchurch, New Zealand—a highly secular society. There was a sudden spike in religiosity in the people who experienced that event, but the rest of the country remained as secular as ever.

As Peter Berger put it: "Modernity does not necessarily produce secularity. It necessarily produces pluralism [. . .] the coexistence in the same society of different world views and value systems." The universal need for comfort in the face of pain and uncertainty means that spirituality and religious belief will continue, albeit in less organized, institutionalized forms. Grace Davie called this "believing without belonging." For instance, in 2012, Ryan Hornbeck found that the online game *World of Warcraft* was assuming spiritual importance for some players in China. Religious belief and practice are increasingly personal, pragmatic, and about direct spiritual experiences and transformation.

CONTROL VERSUS CHAOS

While religion can relate to an external locus of control (e.g. God as a higher power commanding our destiny), religious people often have a strong internal sense of control. Harold Koenig found that those who pray and ask God for guidance feel a sense of control over their own situation, helping them to cope with depression and anxiety.

FAMILY AND MARRIAGE

In anthropology, kinship is the web of social relationships that form an essential part of human life across all societies. Given its universal importance, kinship has been a central tenet in anthropology. As Robin Fox put it in 1967, "Kinship is to anthropology what logic is to philosophy or the nude is to art; it is the basic discipline of the subject." This chapter considers the two main patterns of kinship that are found around the world: family (a form of kin group) and marriage. Families exist in all societies across the world, and they are part of what makes us human. However, how family and marriage are understood varies considerably across cultures, including ideas about how people relate to each other, as well as the ideal form of marriage, parenting styles, childcare responsibilities, and many other family-related matters. You will also be introduced in this chapter to the different forms of family units that are becoming more widely accepted, and legally recognized, in the twenty-first century.

Kinship systems

While families come in all shapes and sizes, anthropologists have identified several broad categories that are often culturally recognized across the world and define the transfer of property or wealth across generations. In **matrilineal societies**, descent is established through the biological link between a mother and child. Women pass on their name and wealth to their daughters (and, in some cases, sons). The mother's brothers provide support and property to the children. Examples of this are the Ashanti people of Ghana and the Khasi people of India. **Patrilineal societies** are those that connect generations through the father's line. This is the most common kinship system across the world. Both kinds of kinship are considered **unilineal**, as they recognize descent or "kin" through only one side of the family, but they do not necessarily reflect the relationships or emotional bonds between people. Families that are defined by descent from both the father's and the mother's sides of the family are known as **bilateral societies**, such as the Javanese people of Indonesia.

MOSUO WOMEN

The Mosuo people of China maintain a matrilineal society. Most political power is in the hands of women and the family matriarch makes all major household decisions. If a heterosexual couple decide to be in a relationship, they have a "walking marriage" that bears no social or economic ties. When they want to meet, the man "walks" to the woman's house and returns home by sunrise. Any children are raised primarily by the mother's family.

Ambilineal descent (otherwise known as cognatic descent) is selective descent, either matrilineally or patrilineally. The decision may be made by each generation, based on the relative wealth and/or importance of the father's and the mother's family lines. This is common among Samoans, Māori, Hawaiians, and the people of the Gilbert Islands.

Some anthropologists, like Laura Fortunato, have disputed the relevance of these kinship terms in the twenty-first century. New expressions are needed to capture more complex social scenarios.

Kinship and care

One of the defining characteristics of our species is the way we love and care for each other. As opposed to the way we quarrel, which is not dissimilar to other species, the way we express affection shows an advanced capacity for kindness and empathy. As early as 1.6 million years ago, there is evidence of our human ancestors taking care of the sick and frail. Caregiving is observed in every human society in the world, and most of it is provided within family relationships or small communities. Kinship roles themselves are often defined, in part, through a person's obligations to or entitlements to care during different stages in life. But there are profound differences about what constitutes proper care and how such care should be distributed within a family (and beyond). Anthropologists encourage us to think about cultural norms regarding the different expectations, rights, and care responsibilities placed on family members. For instance, what does the status of father entail in your culture—is he a primary caregiver, a co-parent, or is the caregiving role limited?

Your brain and kinship

Anthropologists have been studying how the human brain has certain emotional systems and limits for romantic, social, and family networks. One of the reasons our brain is so large in comparison to other species is to allow us to maintain complex social relationships that go beyond our immediate family. In the 1990s, British anthropologist Robin Dunbar developed a theory that humans can maintain stable social relationships of around 150 people—this is known as **"Dunbar's number"** and includes extended family as well as friends. According to Dunbar, this is "the number of people you would not feel embarrassed about joining uninvited for a drink if you happened to bump into them in a bar." However, there is a network hierarchy, with only five out of the 150 considered "intimate" (and to which you likely devote 60 percent of your time). Family is usually prioritized, with friendships requiring more time and investment to maintain emotional attachment. As a result, people with large extended families have been found to have fewer close friendships.

The purpose of marriage

For thousands of years, families consisted of loosely organized groups of up to 30 people. As agricultural societies developed, so did the need for greater stability. The first recorded evidence of marriage ceremonies uniting women and men dates from around 2350 BCE in Mesopotamia. Marriage has since evolved into a widespread institution with various meanings and functions in different cultural contexts, though its primary purpose seems to be consistently practical rather than romantic. Through the institution of marriage, kinship groups (and later, religions) were able to regulate relationships, and specify the rights and obligations expected of two individuals and any offspring they produced. Some anthropologists have argued that marriage is primarily about identifying the "descent" and ownership of children, as well as providing the latter with certain rights, including inheritance. Other functions served by marriage include the regulation of sexual activity and defining rules about when it is appropriate to have children, establishing peoples' economic and social responsibilities, and satisfying the basic human needs of affection and companionship.

Types of marriage

The most common form of marriage around the world, **monogamy**, involves two individuals. This is traditionally referred to as the union of one man and one woman, although an increasing number of countries now recognize same-sex marriages. Monogamy includes having multiple spouses over an individual's lifetime, though only one at a time (known as **serial monogamy**). This is quite common in industrial societies and can arise if a partner dies or in the event of divorce. **Polygamy** is a marriage involving multiple partners, which can fall into two categories:

 polygyny—a marriage involving one man and multiple wives.

 polyandry—a marriage involving one woman and multiple husbands. This is rare but can be found among the Nyinba people of Nepal.

Anthropologists have found several reasons why polygamous marriages can be preferred, including a need for rapid population growth, if the ratio of women to men is very high, to spread the burden of work, increasing care for children, as well as social status.

Who can you marry?

Until very recently in human history, couples married for practical reasons rather than love. This is still the case in much of the world, with **arranged marriages** being standard practice in numerous cultures, including societies in the Middle East and India. This means that a marriage is coordinated between two families and/or professional matchmakers. Unions are usually decided on several factors, such as similar socio-economic backgrounds, occupations, shared religion or ethnicity, or political grounds. Some people choose to have an arranged marriage to alleviate the pressure of finding a partner.

WEDDING TRADITIONS

According to Western wedding traditions, the groom is not supposed to see the bride before the wedding. This ritual stems from arranged marriages, so the groom would not see his bride before the ceremony and potentially call off the wedding if he did not find her attractive.

Marrying for love is known as **companionate marriage**. However, societies that encourage this form of marriage can still place boundaries on who a person can fall in love with. Anthropologists like William Jankowiak and Alex Nelson have shown how material considerations and compatibilities play a part in determining people's willingness to fall in love, and eventually marry. Such rules that encourage marriage within a cultural group are known as **endogamy** and may include religious communities that require members to marry within their circle, or cultures that exert pressure on people to marry a member of the same ethnicity or race, or someone from similar economic or educational backgrounds. Jankowiak and Nelson argue that societies organized around arranged marriages are not so different from those organized around passionate love. As the anthropologist Helen Fisher has explained, the romantic feeling of love is a basic brain system just like fear or anger; it is biological and innate in you. However, "Who you love," she writes, "where you love, how you express your love all have a huge cultural component."

Types of families

A **nuclear family** (also known as a **conjugal family**) comprises a mother and father in a culturally recognized relationship (such as marriage), and their dependent children. This can involve unequal inheritance (absolute nuclear families) or equal inheritance (egalitarian nuclear families). **Non-conjugal families** are those that do have dependent children but don't have parents who are a married couple.

Stem families are extended families with unequal inheritance. This usually means three generations: grandparents, married offspring, and their grandchildren. **Community families** are extended families with equal inheritance. **Blended families** occur when divorced or widowed parents marry, and **families of choice** are families that lack legal recognition (e.g. unmarried).

The cultural traits that shape all these family units are generally slow to change, because they are inherited vertically from parent to child and are regulated by social norms. There are exceptions, though, such as the Yanomami people of Brazil and Venezuela, who live in large communal houses of up to 400 people. They strongly believe in equality, with decisions being made by consensus.

Same-sex marriage

Same-sex couples have existed for centuries, though they have not always been regarded in the same terms as today. As the geneticist Adam Rutherford puts it, "In many examples, it may be better thought of as 'something they did' rather than 'something they are'." There is evidence of marriage between individuals of the same sex from the first century during the Roman Empire, though there was no legal provision for it at the time. More recently, Denmark was the first country to legally recognize same-sex couples in 1989 by establishing registered partnerships. In 2001, the Netherlands was the first country to legalize same-sex marriage.

ENBROTHERMENT

In early modern France, two men could enter a legal contract of "enbrotherment" (*affrèrement*). This allowed civil unions between unrelated male adults who pledged to live together sharing "*un pain, un vin, et une bourse*"—one bread, one wine, and one purse. This legal category may represent the earliest form of sanctioned same-sex union.

Infertility treatments

Kinship and ideas of what constitutes "family" have been changing at a rapid pace since the twentieth century. Same-sex relationships, modern systems of adoption, interracial couples, single-parent households, cohabitation patterns, and reproductive technologies have all widened the scope for what a family can be. The traditional idea of biology determining family has also steadily declined, alongside advances in the field of human reproduction, including IVF, sperm and egg donation, and surrogacy (forms of **assisted reproductive technologies**, or ARTs). As ARTs have developed over time, so have the legal, ethical, social, and cultural responses to them. Technology also allows greater monitoring of pregnancies, with further advances expected in the coming decades. Anthropologists are researching the implications of these technologies on kinship and family, such as the structure of parenthood and inheritance, the race- and class-based barriers in IVF access, questions surrounding genetic engineering and cultural preferences (such as male children being preferred over female), and implications of having a prolonged reproductive lifespan. These changes and controversies will impact families for generations to come.

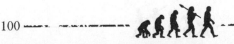

SEX AND GENDER

A lot of what you consider "normal" or "natural" is not grounded in biology and is in fact cultural. One area where these cultural creations exist is with respect to sex and gender. Until the early twentieth century, anthropologists reflected the public perception that the social and political divisions between men and women were "natural." Thanks to the Women's Liberation Movement of the 1970s, a new generation of female anthropologists began to question the gender binaries of the discipline, both in its fieldwork and literature. A distinction between sex and gender began to be identified, which allowed anthropologists to consider different concepts of gender across cultures and time, and how these inform other parts of life. Twenty-first century anthropology is characterized by greater attention to people who identify as transgender or homosexual, or whose identities do not fit into the traditional male/female dichotomy that dominated earlier anthropological work. This chapter challenges you to consider the relevance of culture versus nature in defining gender and sexuality, both personally and within society at large.

Sex vs gender

To understand the role that culture plays in gender identities, we must distinguish between sex and gender. Sex relates to the natural biological and physiological differences between males and females, largely centered on genitalia, reproductive organs, chromosomes, and hormonal profiles. Gender refers to the traits or characteristics that a culture assigns to people based on sex and includes categories beyond the male/female distinction. The two terms are often conflated because, unlike other cultural inventions, gender has a biological component. Anthropologists study how cultures have produced complex and elaborate ideas around gender, creating notions that barely resemble what is natural and innate. One example is **biological determinism**, which was popular until the late twentieth century, and held that social positions are encoded in and determined by sex. In 1889, Patrick Geddes and J. Arthur Thomson argued that political rights should not be extended to women due to their supposed tendency to conserve their surplus energy rather than expend it. Similarly, in the 1970s, some argued that women should not become airline pilots due to their hormonal instability.

The binary model

You may assume that all cultures divide human beings into two genders and that "gender fluidity" is a modern phenomenon. However, anthropologists have observed gender variability across history and around the world. The prevalent scientific view from the Ancient Greeks, until the late 1700s, viewed males and females as two different forms of the same sex category, with the reproductive organs being inside or outside the body, but fundamentally the same. Differences in the social roles of men and women were not necessarily tied to their bodies. It was in the late eighteenth century that scientists began to think of female and male anatomies as radically different. This created the foundations of the binary model of gender that prevailed until the twenty-first century.

CISGENDER

The term cisgender is increasingly used in the twenty-first century and describes a person whose gender identity is the same as their sex assigned at birth.

In some societies, practices that identify people as neither male nor female have existed for centuries. In India, there is a third/sacred gender (*hijra*), while on the Pacific Islands of Samoa, *fa'afafine* have both masculine and feminine traits. The Buginese people of Indonesia recognize three sexes (male, female, and intersex) and five genders (men, women, *calabai*, *calalai*, and *bissu*). *Calabai* are male at birth but adopt traditionally female gender roles, while *calalai* are female at birth but adopt male roles. *Bissu* defy classification and embody the full gender spectrum.

TERMS TO KNOW

Gender expression is how a person presents gender outwardly, through behavior, clothing, or other perceived characteristics.

Gender identity is a person's internal sense of gender, whether man, woman, neither, or both.

Transgender (or trans) refers to people whose gender identity or expression does not conform to their birth-assigned sex.

Non-binary is used by people who do not describe themselves or their genders as fitting into the categories of man or woman.

Two spirits

In many Native American cultures, everything that exists is thought to come from the spirit world. Within this context, anthropologists have identified a widespread phenomenon of "two-spirit" people. This applies to individuals who do not comfortably conform to the gender roles and ideologies normally associated with their biological sex. Intersex (those with ambiguous genitals), androgynous people (those with both characteristics), feminine males, and masculine females have therefore traditionally been held in high regard because they are seen as doubly blessed, having both the spirit of a man and the spirit of a woman. In groups like the Navajo, a *Nádleehi* (literally translated as "one who is transformed") was traditionally prized for their valuable contribution, as they were often artistically gifted and regularly did the work of both men and women. In the twentieth century, there was a marked decline in respect for these individuals, as homophobic European Christian influences increased among many Native Americans. Two-spirit people were forced more and more to conform to society's standard gender roles.

Penalties, honour, and shame

Various cultures impose sanctions and penalties for those that deviate from gender roles and segregation. In smaller communities, family members or neighbours report inappropriate behavior, to other family members. Historically, many cultures have imposed penalties for the sexual freedom or behavior of women who engage in activities that "shame" or dishonour their family. In some cases, gender-based violence or policing is a common response, such as verbal abuse, rape, female genital cutting, and so-called "honour killings." Codes of sexual conduct and penalties for their violation are not exclusive to orthodox sectors of major religions; they can be seen in the stigmatizing and "slut-shaming" practices in Europe and North America, as well as in family beliefs, peer pressure, education, government policies, and the media.

Among the many ways in which states can exert power over the human body, anthropologists look at family planning policies, laws that ban (or permit) contraception and abortion, and programs that promote fertility, including subsidized infertility treatments.

Forced categorization

Babies born with genitals, anatomy or chromosomes that do not fit neatly into male or female categories are sometimes called "intersex." This differs from the old term "hermaphrodite," which refers to bodies that encompass all male and all female organs at once. Intersex births are quite widespread; a study by the Intersex Society of North America found that they comprise one in every 1,666 births. Anthropologists have catalogued how doctors worldwide often act quickly to surgically "fix" babies identified at birth as intersex, by sculpting the body to make it functionally male or female, or using forms of hormone treatments. Interest in the medical standard of care for intersex infants increased since the 1990s, and public awareness and laws to protect intersex children have become more widespread in the twenty-first century. Medical anthropologists like Katrina Karkazis have looked at the conflicts and struggles surrounding the treatment of intersex conditions. Intersexuality also poses a challenge for forensic anthropologists, as the he/she binary is the primary building block of a biological profile (a description of a person's physical characteristics), which may not reflect a person's gender.

Margaret Mead

One of the most influential anthropologists in history, Margaret Mead conducted research into different gender role patterns across various cultures in the 1930s. She conducted field trips to Papua New Guinea, Bali, and the Pacific Islands of Samoa to determine the extent to which temperamental differences between the sexes were innate (i.e. genetically determined) or culturally determined. Her findings suggested that gender roles were socially constructed and not biologically based, and that these roles determined a person's limits and freedoms. Among her many observations, she found a smoother transition to adulthood in societies that exhibited a relaxed attitude toward adolescent sexual activity. Describing the widely varying behavior of men and women in different cultures, from the violent women of the Mundugumors to the nurturing men of the Arapesh tribe (both of Papua New Guinea), Mead maintained that social convention, rather than sex, determines how people behave. Her work directly challenged the prevailing culture that existed in the USA at the time, which was predicated on fixed gender roles and the inferiority of women.

Gender roles

Gender can be experienced across the world in a variety of ways, due to the "gender roles" that different cultures assign to the male and female sexes; they are culturally specific. Another way to understand this is to consider **gender stereotypes**, which refer to the preconceived ideas that a culture has about what is appropriate and acceptable behavior for males and females. An example is the notion that boys are "tough" and girls are "nurturing." Gender roles influence a wide range of human behaviors and decision-making, including clothing, choice of occupation, and a person's intimate relationships.

EQUALITY IN PRACTICE

Anthropologist Shanshan Du's book, *Chopsticks Only Work in Pairs* (2002), shows how a complementary and equal gender system exists within the Lahu people of Southwest China, where a male–female pair historically took responsibility for local leadership. Male–female dyads (meaning pairs) completed daily household tasks in tandem and worked together in the fields.

Gender stratification describes an unequal distribution of rewards between men and women, reflecting their different positions in a social hierarchy. Rewards can include socially valued resources, power, and personal freedom. Many societies continue to uphold binary gender systems and inequality; in Saudi Arabia, women were prohibited from driving until 2018 and remain subject to a "modest" dress code, as well as male guardianship laws regarding marriage, employment, and travel. Anthropologists also consider how gender roles can be sources of empowerment. For instance, in various societies women can establish their own ritual practices, personal investments or savings schemes, or social and educational centers.

MENSTRUATION

Some societies view menstrual blood as polluting or impure (such as Orthodox Jews); others view it as a cause for celebration. Among the Sambia people of Papua New Guinea, men take part in nose-bleeding rituals when their wives menstruate. In Fiji, some communities lay out a special mat for girls on their first period and a special feast (*tunudra*) is prepared.

Sexuality

Humans engage in a wide range of sexual behaviors, all linked to our physical and cultural evolution. While sexuality (sexual feelings and attraction) is universal, anthropologists focus on the ways in which sexuality and sexual behavior are interpreted and experienced across the world, as well as the differences between us and animals. For instance, human sexuality clearly serves a purpose beyond reproduction. Unlike other mammals, human females are sexually receptive throughout the year, regardless of fertility status. Sexual relationships with people of the same sex have been recorded among the Ancient Greeks, indigenous people of the Americas, the samurai warriors of Japan, and many other historical cultures.

DEFINING SEX

Whether an act is considered sexual or not is determined by the cultural context. Anthropologists working in certain African societies, such as the one in Lesotho of South Africa, have observed that sex is restricted to contact between a penis and a vulva. Genital contact between members of the same sex is not considered to be sex.

Heteronormativity is the idea that binary gender identity and heterosexuality are the "normal" and preferred modes of sexual orientation. It results in often-unnoticed systems of rights and privileges accompanying sexual and marital relations between males and females. Cultural ideas about what is "normal" or "natural" also extend to sexual positions, the desire for orgasms, the ways sexuality is discussed with children, and numerous sexual practices, such as masturbation, oral sex, anal sex, and sex during menstruation. The anthropologist Kath Weston has highlighted the problem in transposing Western terminologies onto sexual practices and identities in other parts of the world. For instance, married couples within the Aka and Ngandu people of Central Africa view sex as "work of the night," with consistent reports of intercourse multiple times a night. Masturbation and homosexuality are virtually unknown and there are no equivalent terms for them in their language. In making these observations, Barry and Bonnie Hewlett have noted that the Western custom of sleeping through the night suggests that daytime employment is prioritized over sex.

MIGRATION

One of the defining features of the twenty-first century is migration, and many anthropologists specialize in identifying patterns, solutions, and problems that can affect migrants today. Because anthropology traditionally focused on small-scale localities, human migration only became a subject of interest in the 1950s. It has since become an enormous field of study, with the cultural and social dimensions of migration increasingly taking precedence over the earlier economic one. This chapter looks at some of the key questions and concerns that anthropologists have raised. You will gain insights about how and why humans have migrated throughout history, and the effect that this has had on our species. Terms that are common in the public domain, such as "indigenous" and "refugee," will also be clarified, alongside the challenges and misunderstandings that anthropology seeks to address. Issues tackled earlier in this book—such as identity, communication, and family—are relevant to consider within the context of migration, as anthropologists often focus their research on one or more of these elements.

What is migration?

Migration is the movement of people from one place to another, with the intention of resettlement. The media often presents a misleading image of unprecedented migration across countries that is far from historical fact. Mobility is something that has characterized our species for thousands of years, from the initial human colonization of Sahul (Australia, New Guinea, Tasmania and the Aru Islands) about 40,000 years ago—the earliest movement of Palaeolithic hunter-gatherers 15,000 years ago—to the merchants travelling from the East and West along the Silk Road and the millions who travelled from Europe to the USA in the nineteenth century. The proportion of people migrating has also remained constant, with increased numbers simply reflecting the rise in global population. What *has* changed is the ability of people travelling or settling in different locations to remain connected to their family and friends, cheaply and easily, and the opportunities to cover greater distances. Travel for non-migration purposes, such as tourism or work, also increased exponentially during the twentieth century.

Transport and technology

In the 1880s, E. G. Ravenstein posited a theory of human migration contending that most migrants move short distances, usually to large cities. Since that time, advances in transportation, reduced costs of travel, and improvements in communication technology have made migration across regions and nation states more viable. Anthropologists now consider the ways people travel and settle into their new locations, the extent to which contact is maintained with loved ones, and whether capital is sent back home to relatives. Occupational shifts, such as the movement from agriculture to manufacturing and services, are also tracked. The anthropologist Aihwa Ong used the term "flexible citizenship" in relation to the transnational movement of Hong Kong's business elite—an idea that is increasingly relevant for a huge range of occupations in the twenty-first century.

> If a migrant worker sends resources back to their home country (usually money), these are known as remittances, and they are integral to the economic systems of lower- and middle-income countries.

Why people move

A "migrant" is someone who leaves their country of residence and settles into a different country (permanently or temporarily). It is likely that you have heard the term "migrant workers," and this refers to individuals who move from one country to another for the purpose of employment. However, migration is not always voluntary; every year, millions are forced to flee their homes due to a huge range of factors, such as natural disasters, persecution, or armed conflict. Many anthropologists focus their efforts on trying to understand migration experiences and the many reasons why people migrate, both historically and in the present day.

- **Colonization** occurs when nation states expand and occupy other territories, establishing political and economic control over colonized people.

- **Diaspora** refers to people moving abroad and remaining deeply connected with their home cultures (e.g. "work diaspora" for employment purposes and "trade diaspora" looking for new markets).

- **Enslavement** involves slave trades and human trafficking.

- 🐒 **Forced displacement and resettlement** refers to the movement of people against their will.

- 🐒 **Nomadism** is the movement of communities across long distances in cyclical patterns.

- 🐒 **Refuge** is the condition of a migrant fleeing from intolerable conditions (of a political or ideological nature) or human rights violations, avoiding forced taxation or conscription, or escaping military conquest or war.

- 🐒 **Territorial expansion** happens when populations move beyond their geographic margins.

- 🐒 **Labor migrants** are individuals seeking employment, including positions that many nations label with terms like "higher" skilled (such as the financial industries) or "lower" skilled (such as construction or agriculture).

It is possible for the labor force of a country to be comprised almost entirely of international migrants. For instance, the proportions of migrant-to-local workers in Bahrain, Kuwait, Qatar, and the United Arab Emirates are among the highest in the world.

Borders and boundaries

All migration is characterized by borders. These are geographical limits that separate countries, states, provinces, counties, cities, and so on, which restrict the freedom of people to travel and migrate. Very few borders follow natural geographic features, such as rivers or mountain ranges (e.g. the Pyrenees mountains between Spain and France); most are artificially created for political or economic purposes. As well as determining land ownership, borders also separate political/governmental bodies and decide the citizenship of individuals. They shape people's sense of identity, belonging, and culture. Once a line is drawn, nations are often unwilling to relinquish such borders.

A KURDISH STATE

Kurds are the largest ethnic group in the world without their own nation state and with no legal standing as members of the United Nations. There are roughly 35 million Kurds living throughout Turkey, Iran, Iraq, Syria, and Armenia.

Borders are closely tied to the idea of boundaries, which anthropologists perceive as social constructs. These boundaries influence human behavior and thinking, as well as the symbolic and cultural differences across them, such as class, gender, race, etc. The formation and upkeep of boundaries themselves have also become a focus of study, as in the case of the frontiers that divided the Indian subcontinent, forming Pakistan in 1947 and Bangladesh in 1971. The research of Willem van Schendel and Ellen Bal shows how the creation of these boundaries led to the exclusion of ethnic communities, such as the Chakmas and the Garo Christians, from mainstream society.

Unequal mobility

In the twenty-first century, the opportunities available for work abroad are often determined by your nationality, level of education, skill set, and socio-economic background, which place you in categories of border entry and settlement. If you are "higher skilled," you can enjoy access to competitive markets such as the USA. On the other hand, sponsorship-based employment (known as *kafala*) in countries like Saudi Arabia and Oman restricts the ability of migrant workers to change jobs or leave the country without their employers' permission.

The language used by the media to describe immigrants and the hostility or hospitality that they experience in their everyday life are also rich sources of study. For instance, an expatriate (or "expat") is defined as someone who temporarily resides outside of their native country for work purposes. There is no difference between an expat and a migrant, particularly if the latter does return to their home country (known as "reverse migration"). The different words can be seen to reflect the role that race and class play in the subject of migration.

Voluntary vs forced migration

Anthropologists have often structured the study of migration and diaspora within a framework of push and pull factors. Push factors are those that drive people away from their home countries, usually forced by external circumstances such as natural disasters, war, oppression, climate change, and so on. Pull factors attract people to a new home, usually encouraged by internal aspirations for an improved quality of life, such as better working conditions or wages, job opportunities, educational prospects, or improved healthcare. However, the decision to migrate is often multi-layered and complex, so this binary framework has been critiqued for being too automated, passive, and simplistic. Hein de Haas has attempted to redefine human mobility as people's freedom to choose where to live—including the option to stay—and has given greater consideration to structural factors, such as social inequality. For instance, forms of labor that are often seen as exploitative due to low wages and job insecurity (such as undocumented migration from Mexico to the USA or Indonesia to Malaysia) can still be beneficial due to the increase in family income, education opportunities, or access to healthcare.

The meaning of "indigenous"

"Indigenous" can have different meanings: arguably, the human species is indigenous to Africa, and Pacific Islands communities have indigenous marine knowledge. The phrase "indigenous people" is debated, and some countries prefer "tribes," "First Peoples/Nations," or "aboriginals." They are the descendants of the earliest known inhabitants of a region, with distinct cultural traditions linked to its land and natural resources. There are 370–500 million indigenous people worldwide, in 90 countries. Examples include the Quechua people of Peru and the Zulus of South Africa.

The ceremonial war dance of the Māori people is known as *Haka*, and there are different types. The most well-known is *Ka Mate* (composed around 1820 by chief Te Rauparaha), which is performed by the All Blacks rugby team and celebrates life triumphing over death. Although *Haka* was traditionally performed by men before going to war or when two groups came together, it is now used for various social occasions, including birthdays, weddings, or funerals.

Diaspora

People living across the world who share a common national or ethnic origin are known as diaspora. The term was originally used to describe the forced dispersal of Jewish, Greek, and Armenian people, but it has expanded to encompass voluntary forms of migration and populations connected by a common culture or language. Even those who share a special affection for a country, without any family origins in it, can be grouped together as "affinity diaspora." The characteristics, behaviors, and host country integration of diaspora are fascinating areas of study for migration anthropologists. Today, developments in communication technology have transformed the experience of diaspora compared to that of previous generations. International postal services, instant messaging, and video calling mean that memory and ritual practice are no longer the prevailing ways used to maintain identity and culture. For instance, the research of Daniel Miller and Don Slater in 2000 showed how internet access enabled Trinidadians (or "Trinis") living around the world to maintain their culture, language, and connection online, such as through chat rooms and virtual "liming" (relaxing or hanging out).

Refugees

To be recognized as a refugee, an individual (known as an **asylum seeker**) must prove a well-founded fear of persecution in their home country because of their race, religion, nationality, membership in a particular social group, or political opinion (according to the 1951 Convention Relating to the Status of Refugees). According to customary international law, refugees should also not be returned, or **refouled**, to a country where they fear persecution. Unlike migrant workers, refugees cannot go back safely to their country of origin. Despite media images that seem to indicate the contrary, refugees comprise a small proportion of all migrants and the vast majority live in the Global South. There is a great deal of anthropological research into the ways in which refugees rebuild lives for themselves while retaining their cultural origins, as well as the ethical questions raised by government policies of security and border control in the face of humanitarian crises. For instance, Didier Fassin has looked at the gradual change in French society's perception of asylum seekers, to the extent that "selective humanitarianism has replaced legal entitlement."

THE
MODERN DAY

One of the features that distinguishes humans from animals is the ability to think about different options and make decisions accordingly. It could be argued that the alternative realities facing our species in the twenty-first century are the most challenging and urgent in all human history. Climate change, extremism, social inequality, and technological advances have all been accelerating at a speed that is unparalleled and perhaps untenable for the wellbeing or survival of humanity and Earth. As a discipline that spans the sciences, arts, and humanities, anthropology can provide unique insights and solutions to these problems. This chapter introduces you to the latest anthropological studies, the new techniques being used to conduct research and communicate findings, as well as the vital role that anthropology can play in the resolution of our species' most pressing problems. This includes an overview of how technology and artificial intelligence are shaping culture and redefining what it means to be human, the emergence of new fields of anthropology, and the effect that globalization is having on different societies.

Money and exchange

Some anthropologists assert that money is one of the greatest "tools" created by modern humans. Yuval Noah Harari has gone so far as saying, "Money is the only trust system created by humans that can bridge almost any cultural gap, and that does not discriminate." Rather than being dismissed as the root of all evil, money provided the means for resources to be exchanged and for collaboration across societies. With over 90 percent of all money now being in the form of electronic data (rather than physical cash), the cultural symbolism and rituals surrounding money continue to evolve and provide a fascinating research area for anthropologists. In the wake of the internet, technological developments, increasing mobility, as well as inflation and political instability in numerous countries, convenience and security have become the key priorities for most buyers and consumers (whether on an individual or corporate level). In the twenty-first century, the growing presence of cryptocurrencies and non-fungible tokens (NFTs) will no doubt play a part in reshaping our understanding and habits regarding ownership and money.

Digital anthropology

Digital anthropology examines the relationship between humans and digital technology. This field is so new that its name is yet to be finalized! You may come across it in different guises, such as techno-anthropology, digital ethnography, cyberanthropology, or virtual anthropology, but the objective is the same: to analyze and critique digital technology from a social and cultural perspective. This covers the whole range of digital phenomena, from social media to 3D printing, algorithms, data, and digital infrastructures. The core theories laid out earlier in this book (like identity and communication) are studied within the context of digital culture. The social and regional impacts of technology are considered, as well as its reach and adoption within different societies.

RESEARCHING THE VIRTUAL

Anthropologists conducting virtual fieldwork are often invisible, leaving no trace of their research on blogs or websites, or assuming anonymous names in chat forums. To relay their findings, they group together their research participants (e.g. social media accounts or bloggers), without identification.

What is perhaps surprising is that traditional methods of research can still be used by anthropologists. Participant observation is achieved by joining online communities to learn about their customs and world views, and private interviews, historical research, and the gathering of quantitative data are still conducted by some.

However, anthropologists disagree about whether online research alone is sufficient or if research can only be considered complete when the subjects are studied holistically, both online and offline. Some anthropologists, like Tom Boellstorff, argue that it is necessary to engage with subjects "in their own terms." He likens it to fieldwork in physical locations, with a similar need to understand new languages, traditions, and numerous codes of behavior. Others, such as Jenna Burrell, say that the subject's life outside the internet is also relevant. For instance, when presenting her research into the young people of Ghana who became online scammers, Burrell included their everyday reality of poverty and exclusion, in order to broaden our understanding and challenge preconceptions.

Memes

The term "meme" was invented by evolutionary biologist Richard Dawkins to refer to any cultural entity that an observer might consider a replicator; put simply, it's an idea that is repeated and copied, and becomes part of a culture. Memes have been likened to cultural genes, as they self-replicate, mutate, and respond to social pressures.

Internet memes, which are usually for entertainment or comedy purposes, are an example of Dawkins' meme theory at work, in the sense of how they reflect current cultural events and become part of how a time period is defined. Some call it a process of "micro-evolution," with memes passing from person to person until they start trending. Once replicated, they remain in the "meme pool" of culture. For an anthropologist, internet memes are cultural barometers with a great deal of meaning: helping us to see trends, and understand the way we think and talk, as well as shaping culture. Individuals can become cultural icons with worldwide fame in a matter of hours. Memes are cultural artifacts for the twenty-first century.

Virtual worlds

The twenty-first century has seen the increasing rise of virtual spaces, whether for work or social purposes, with anthropological methods being adapted to explore these "subcultures." They include video games, social media platforms and live chats, and video-calling software that allows dozens of people to meet from anywhere in the world. Relationships are now forged online among people with common interests, including shared ethnicity, religion, former residence, or occupation. Many anthropologists focus their work on trying to understand these virtual societies and challenge the notion that these cyber spaces are not real. The lack of a tangible, physical form does not undermine the *real* relationships that are created and sustained.

YOUTUBE

Anthropologist Patricia G. Lange has considered video-sharing cultures and the emotions that motivate users, as well as the impact of losing control over what is shared. She explained how key concepts from anthropology—participant observation, reciprocity, and community—applied to YouTube.

Artificial intelligence

Originally coined by the American scientist John McCarthy in 1955, the term artificial intelligence (AI) refers to problem-solving and decision-making capabilities in computers and machines. Without necessarily being aware of it, you are likely to be surrounded by AI, such as email spam filters, your smartphone, loan applications, song or movie recommendations on media apps, smart assistants (like Alexa, Siri, etc.), and so on. For the moment, AI is designed to perform specific tasks, but without any ability to reprogram or improve itself. From an anthropological perspective, the conundrum presented by AI is whether it is redefining what it means to be human. As such, technology companies need to identify the core values they wish to protect for users. For instance, algorithms on numerous social media platforms have contributed to the spread of conspiracy theories, fake news, and alt-right videos. Posts or videos with high engagement levels (which tend to be the most controversial and emotional) are automatically recommended. Anthropologists can help to develop "ethical AI" by understanding the social context in which these technologies are designed and deployed.

Human biology

Traditional ideas regarding humans as superior or separate from animals have steadily been dismantled. In the twenty-first century, biological anthropologists are finding increasing evidence of our similarities to animals, as well as explanations for modern human diversity. Continuous fossil discoveries, coupled with advances in dating techniques, are allowing anthropologists to piece together a clearer picture of early hominin evolution; a new species of human ancestor was discovered as recently as 2021 (the *Homo bodoensis*). Poor nutrition and disease in the Global South are also subjects of study that are often combined between anthropologists and scientists.

Human proximity to animals can lead to cross-species transmission of viruses (known as zoonotic diseases), such as Covid-19. According to the research of Martine Peeters and her colleagues, it is likely that HIV/AIDS originally jumped from chimpanzees and gorillas to humans when carcasses were butchered for meat. Some anthropologists look at traditional practices and local knowledge to anticipate future pandemics.

An evolving discipline

With the advancement of technology, and increasing exchanges between different cultures and knowledge systems, anthropology has been steadily expanding its application beyond its traditional fields and methods. One sub-discipline that is relatively new is the science of human identification, known as forensic anthropology. This is often for legal or medical purposes—for instance, if a police investigation needs to confirm the identity of a body, a forensic anthropologist will be called upon to create a biological profile of the deceased that includes ancestry, sex, age at death, and stature. They are also employed by museums, universities, and private companies providing private forensic services.

Another growing area of interest is multispecies ethnography, which is a research method that acknowledges the interconnectedness and inseparability of humans and all other life forms. While conventional ethnography is centered on human cultures, this approach seeks to expand our understanding of the environment in which humans live, and includes the study of animals, plants, fungi, and microbes.

Donna Haraway, one of the pioneers of multispecies ethnography, wrote, "If we appreciate the foolishness of human exceptionalism, then we know that becoming is always becoming *with*, in a contact zone where the outcome, where who is in the world, is at stake."

In a similar vein, anthropology is turning its attention to climate change, pollution, species extinctions, and habitat destruction. Many anthropologists look at how individuals experience and adapt to climate change, as well as the accessibility and social inequality issues posed by environmental resources. Some focus their research on environmental racism, where injustice occurs within a racial context, whether in practice or policy. For instance, Nick Shapiro examined the contaminated trailers distributed to (mostly) African American residents affected by Hurricane Katrina in 2005.

ANTHROPOCENE

The term Anthropocene is used by anthropologists and scientists to refer to the geological age in which human activity has been the dominant influence on climate and the environment.

Globalization

Global trade links have existed since the Han dynasty of China opened for international business in 130 BCE, but globalization, as we understand it today, only came about in the 1990s. Put simply, it is the interdependence of the world's cultures, populations, and economies through the free movement of goods, services, and capital. For an anthropologist, the interest lies in the interaction between different cultures, and the rapid changes that globalization brings to the movement of money and capital, migration, tourism, and the exchange of cultures across societies. This has also led to a change in the theories that dominate anthropology; rather than focusing on kinship and social organizations, the more relevant and universal topics in the twenty-first century are social inequality, identity politics, and transnationalism. Anthropologists do not assume that globalization is natural and inevitable. They conduct their research with an awareness that the process and experience of globalization are different for every person and region of the world.

Public anthropology

The phrase "off the verandah" is often attributed to Bronisław Malinowski as a call for his fellow anthropologists to move "out of their armchairs" and into the everyday life of their subjects. A century later, this attitude has advanced into a desire to move the discipline of anthropology beyond the academic realm and into the hands of the public. Unlike applied anthropology, which has its roots in colonialism and governance, public anthropology is concerned with expanding the discipline's relevance and audience beyond its traditional academic circles. Anthropologists are aware of the irony that only a tiny portion of society are accessing research that aims to expand our understanding of humanity. One technique emerging for anthropologists to reach wider audiences is through ethnographic film-making, with an early example being the documentary *The Kayapo: Out of the Forest*. Made with the assistance of anthropologist Terry Turner, this shows the Kayapo people of the Amazonian rainforest trying to protect their land.

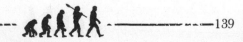

Conclusion

During the eighteenth century, a publication released in France, called the *Encyclopédie*, attempted to put all the world's knowledge into 18,000 pages. In the twenty-first century, the idea that any book, or even the internet, could capture all human wisdom and experience throughout history is absurd. Likewise, any book about anthropology cannot fully reflect a discipline that studies humankind—but this is part of anthropology's appeal. As a species of infinite diversity and potential, as well as inequality and conflict, anthropology inspires human curiosity instead of confrontation, and humility rather than pride. Gillian Tett has said that the world needs a second type of AI: "anthropology intelligence" to see the "bigger picture," to make mental connections, and provide innovative solutions to the challenges we face. By seeing the value in alternative ways of thinking and being, anthropology can help humanity to communicate and collaborate, not despite but *because of* our differences. As Marcel Proust put it: "The real voyage of discovery consists not in seeing new landscapes, but in having new eyes."

Further reading

David P. Barash, *Homo Mysterious: Evolutionary Puzzles of Human Nature* (2012)

Matthew Engelke, *Think Like an Anthropologist* (2017)

David Graeber and David Wengrow, *The Dawn of Everything: A New History of Humanity* (2021)

Joy Hendry and Simon Underdown, *Anthropology: A Beginner's Guide* (2013)

Joseph Henrich, *The Weirdest People in the World: How the West Became Psychologically Peculiar and Particularly Prosperous* (2020)

Johannes Krause and Thomas Trappe, *A Short History of Humanity: How Migration Made Us Who We Are* (2021)

Jeremy MacClancy, *Exotic No More: Anthropology for the Contemporary World* (2019)

Yuval Noah Harari, *Sapiens: A Brief History of Humankind* (2014)

Simon Roberts, *The Power of Not Thinking: How Our Bodies Learn and Why We Should Trust Them* (2020)

Adam Rutherford, *The Book of Humans: A Brief History of Culture, Sex, War and the Evolution of Us* (2018)

Gillian Tett, *Anthro-Vision: How Anthropology Can Explain Business and Life* (2021)

Rebecca Wragg Sykes, *Kindred: Neanderthal Life, Love, Death and Art* (2021)

THE LITTLE BOOK OF
PHILOSOPHY

Rachel Poulton

£6.99
Paperback
ISBN: 978-1-78685-808-5

If you want to know your Socrates from your Sartre and your Confucius from your Kant, this approachable little book will introduce you to the key thinkers, themes and theories you need to know to understand how human ideas have sculpted the world we live in and the way we think today.

THE LITTLE BOOK OF
PSYCHOLOGY

Emily Ralls and
Caroline Riggs

£6.99

Paperback

ISBN: 978-1-78685-807-8

If you want to know your Freud from your Jung and your Milgram from your Maslow, this approachable little book will take you on a whirlwind tour of the key thinkers, themes and theories you need to know to understand how the study of mind and behaviour has sculpted the world we live in and the way we think today.

THE LITTLE BOOK OF PSYCHOLOGY

Emily Ralls and
Caroline Riggs

$6.99
Paperback
ISBN 978-1-63228-085-5

If you want to know your id from your ego and your
Althusser from your Skinner, this accessible little book
will take you on a whistlestop tour of the key thinkers,
theories and discoveries you need to know to understand
the workings of mind and behaviour that sculpted the world
we live in and the way we think today.